ON THE JOB
With God
The Awakening

ON THE JOB
With God
The Awakening

By
JOEL JONES

Higgins
Publishing

OAKLAND, CA

Higgins Publishing Since 2002
Copyright 2014 – Higgins Publishing

Library of Congress Control Number Cataloging in Publication
ISBN 978-0-9815202-8-5

Higgins Publishing, its logos and marks are service marks of
Higgins Publishing

Purchase physical copies online at:
HTTP://WWW.HIGGINSPUBLISHING.COM

DEDICATION

*This book is in dedication to my Lord and Savior
Jesus Christ. How can I thank You Lord...for
coming to the scrap yards of life and collecting a
junk car like me?*

*Thank You for gathering my wife, and I,
rebuilding and restoring us.
Mere words cannot express how thankful we are to
God for putting us on the proper road...the road of
righteousness; to be used as reliable vehicles and
vessels of honor, for the kingdom.*

TABLE OF CONTENTS

INTRODUCTION

Hello, my name is Pastor Joel Jones. At the time of this writing, I am the senior pastor of Spirit of Truth Church Worldwide located in Crockett, CA. My wife of 37 years is Pastor AnnaLisa Jones. We have been pastors for only seven months now. Our church is a new church, and in the natural one would say that my wife and I are the founding pastors, which we are. But what is remarkable is that although on paper and in human terms AnnaLisa and I both founded Spirit of Truth Church Worldwide, in reality it was God who planted this church. The fact that I am even preparing this manuscript is taking place only through His grace and divine guidance. Our church was planned and conceived by our Abba Father before the foundation of the world. You see, my wife and I never planned to even be minister*s*, let alone founding pastors of a church, but then we never planned on any of the things to occur in our lives that have occurred since 2004. But God did! You see, that was the year that God decided to enter our lives in quite an amazing way, a wondrous and supernatural way, proving that *Jesus Christ is the same, yesterday, today, and forever* (Heb13:8).

I have been a Christ follower only since that fateful day in 2004 when the Lord decided that He would reveal Himself to my wife and me. It has now been approximately eight years since the Lord came to us. Before then, I did not know the Lord, and had never even read one verse of the bible. I had only heard bits and pieces of information about a man named Jesus, who for some reason, many people believed to be God.

So, not only did I not know Jesus, but I did not believe Him to be God. And since I had no knowledge of this Jesus, I thought Him to be at best, maybe a prophet and/or a "good man." Boy, was I in for a big surprise!!

The Lord came to my wife and I simultaneously and revealed Himself to us in such a miraculous way that our lives were instantly changed.

In Romans 12:1-2 the Apostle Paul says,

"I beseech you brethren by the mercies of God, to present your bodies as a living sacrifice, holy and acceptable to God, which is our reasonable service. And be not conformed to this world, but be transformed by the renewing of your minds, that you may prove what is that good, and acceptable, and perfect will of God."

So compelling was our transformation that we willingly embarked on a free-falling, no-holds-barred journey, with the Lord leading us. This journey with Jesus has absolutely consumed our lives, making everything else secondary and giving credence to Paul's reasoning in Phil 3:7, *"What things were once gain, I now count as loss for Christ."*

Since meeting the Lord in 2004, He has taken us to His secret place, to the inner recesses of His heavenly realm, revealing to us things that we would never -- nor could ever -- have imagined were it not for His grace, love, and divine hand on our lives. Subsequently, our lives, as well as the lives of countless others have been, and continue to be blessed and changed for the better.

At the time of this writing, I am nearing the end of a 30-year law enforcement career. Most of my law enforcement career has been in the capacity of a police officer, as well as in the role of a sergeant with both the Police Department and (in later years) with the Sheriff's Department. I am currently a sergeant serving with the San Francisco Sheriff's Dept. My wife AnnaLisa worked mainly in medical care and in the retail field before meeting and submitting to the Lord. So you could say that the aforementioned occupations were our formal jobs before the Lord came to us. We are both college educated and have also been heavily involved in music, theater and film acting, and sports and fitness throughout our entire lives. But please do not confuse these occupations and hobbies with what my wife and I truly do in life, for they are only titles. Since 2004, our true work is the work we do for the Lord. We are now *On the Job with God.*

While we are passionate about serving the Lord, we don't take our jobs in the world lightly. Pastor AnnaLisa and I have always been conscientious and hard workers wherever we've served, but you need to understand that we are bondservants of Christ, first and foremost. We have been blessed by the great I AM to have a deep relationship with Him, where He walks with us and speaks to us daily, directing our lives. God saw fit to send angels to AnnaLisa and me to prepare us for what is to come. It didn't matter if we believed in these angels or not, but the fact is, they arrived and communicated with us just the same, informing us that Jesus would soon visit us.

The Lord did just that, manifesting Himself to us and has since shown us many miracles, both tangible, as well as those which took place after AnnaLisa and I had received visions, dreams, and revelations. He has escorted us to the third heaven, as well as to the doorway of outer darkness, where there is surely biting, *weeping and the gnashing of teeth* (Matt 8: 12, 24: 50, 51). The Lord has used, and continues to use us as vessels of honor in healing the sick, casting out demons, and yes, even as He raised a child from the dead. In this case, a young boy had been hit by a car and was dead for at least 40 minutes. Although doctors had given up on him, God told me to

XIII

go to this boy's location in the emergency room of the hospital and pray for him.

Although I was new in the Lord at the time, and was a bit nervous about His command, I knew I was in God's presence, and that I was truly hearing from God. So I did as I was told. Upon standing about 5-7 feet away from the child, and (in direct company of a nurse) I began praying for Jesus to raise him up. And wouldn't you know it…upon voicing Jesus' name, this child's heart began to beat, and his eyes opened shortly thereafter. Needless to say, near chaos ensued on that day inside of the hospital emergency room. To many people this is unheard of. But when you walk with Jesus this is expected.

Jesus declares these things to transpire in Mark 16:17-18,

"And these signs will follow those who believe: In My name they will cast out demons; they will speak with new tongues; they will take up serpents; and if they drink

*anything deadly, it will by no means hurt them; they will
lay hands on the sick, and they will recover."*

This concept is explained further in John 14:12,
and elsewhere throughout the Bible,

*"Most assuredly, I say to you, he who believes in
Me, the works that I do he will do also; and greater works
than these he will do, because I go to My Father."*

Ironically, no more than 8 years ago I never would
have walked into that hospital room to pray that prayer,
because I didn't know the Lord back then. That was
before God had revealed Himself to my wife and me.
How and/or why this happened to AnnaLisa and I can
only completely be answered by Almighty God Himself.
I can only tell you what I know from what the Lord has
seen fit to reveal to two normal people who God has
chosen to be vessels for His plan and purpose. With that,
I will now (under the leading of Jesus Christ my Savior)
share our story *On the Job with God: the Awakening,* with
you.

CHAPTER ONE

THE LEAST OF THESE

Before 2004, we lived what we believed to be a "normal" life. AnnaLisa and I were both born and raised in Illinois on the south side of Chicago. We both attended Wendell Phillips High School and met at the age of 14 near the end of our freshman year of high school. We have been together for about 42 years now. I should tell you that back then AnnaLisa's given name was Denise Randle (more about that later). What happened in our lives beginning in the late summer of 2004 is something so incredible that at times I still find myself crying as I ponder the awesome reality that the Creator of the world...Elohim...the God of Abraham, Isaac, and Jacob, the great I AM...Jesus our Savior has seen fit to take two ordinary people like us on such an amazing supernatural walk with Him, and use us in extraordinary ways and inexplicable circumstances; all according to His plan and purpose. After reading this book you will understand the absolute power and dominion that our Lord, the Creator

1

has over the universe and of course our lives, allowing us to live life liberated and without fear because of "oneness" with Him.

I am confident that readers will come to understand that doors are opened supernaturally when one totally submits to the Lord.

"Leaving the 99 to save the one who has gone astray."

Another amazing thing readers need to know about my walk with Christ is that I was raised in a "culturally Islamic" household. I say "culturally" simply because my parents were followers of Elijah Muhammad and the Nation of Islam. They had journeyed in religion, and had been Jehovah's Witnesses down south in Mississippi and Tennessee for a time. This was long before I was born. They were simple laborers and sharecroppers.

My parents were hard working people, and eventually migrated north to Chicago Illinois, in search of a better way of life. Upon settling on Chicago's south side my parents, still seeking to find their place and serve God, were embraced by the Nation of Islam and eventually became members, serving devoutly. My parents had an already large and steadily growing family. At that time they had at least seven children, and would eventually bring six more into the world. My father found work in Illinois and worked three jobs as a laborer, while my mother cleaned houses mostly in the suburb of Skokie, Illinois. I believe they are now called domestic workers.

I was the 12th of their 13 children. My mother birthed me in Chicago when she was 41 years old. Mama – as we all affectionately called her – once told me that she had so many children that the doctors and midwives forbade her to have any more, saying that doing so would be detrimental to her as well as the child. Still, she gave birth to two more babies (myself and my little brother), both healthy. I now know that everything was planned by the Lord, and that Satan did not want me to be born because God was going to use my wife and me as a team, vessels against the forces of darkness.

Out of the 13 children my mother birthed, she had four 10-pound babies and one 13-pound infant, all via natural childbirth. Looking back, I am sure that might have been a feat possibly deserving of recording in the *Guinness Book of World Records*. No matter, God has it recorded somewhere in His book I'm sure. My mother was one of the gentlest people I have ever known, but she was also tough and resilient. Mama told me that in those days as sharecroppers, she had to be back in the field within an hour after giving birth to resume picking cotton if she wanted to earn her much-needed wages.

While my parents and older siblings followed the urban Muslim doctrine, the last four children were not held to the religion so tightly. In retrospect, I believe that by the time I was born, my parents were simply too exhausted and did not have the energy to raise their last four children with the same zest and control which they had with the previous nine. The first nine children were much older than us and were raised quite differently than we were. By that I mean that they were required to obey the strict rules set forth in the Nation of Islam's community, and even to attend its grade school. The first children were not allowed to participate in sports, as this was against the Nation's doctrine during those early years. However, the later siblings and I were allowed to attend regular public schools, participate in sports, etc. It would be through sports that I would receive a full athletic scholarship and thus leave home and attend college, venturing out of the state of Illinois. But more than that, in retrospect I now see that God had a plan in place all along to insure that I would not be bound by religion that was conceived by man.

AnnaLisa's background is a little different than mine. Not only was she raised in the church, but her family lived in an apartment situated over a church in a building on the west side of Chicago. She also was raised in a large household, with thirteen brothers and sisters. Her parents were both alcoholics and as is common in most families, the devil was busy and there were dysfunctions. AnnaLisa's parents were separated for most of her life as a child, and many times the children had to practically raise themselves. At the tender age of 8 years old, AnnaLisa (whose given name was Denise) was crying out to the Lord as a young recipient of the Holy Spirit of God. Her sisters today still recall that there were times when they were sick that they would call for Denise to pray for them. Little Denise would also actively attempt to evangelize in her neighborhood, rounding up the children, asking them to attend church with her.

Romans 8:30 says,

"Moreover whom He predestined, these He also called; whom He called, these He also justified; and whom He justified, these He also glorified."

Who knew that the hand of God was on Denise? Satan was to have his way with her and her family until the time came for God to reclaim her.

When the family moved to the south side of Chicago, Denise, still a preteen, would beg for someone to take her across town so that she could attend the only church she knew, which was miles away, on the west side of town.

6

As the years passed however, she and I met, and her hunger for the Lord was replaced by her love for me. As is the case in the lives of many young lovers, the female follows the male, and his way of life. This is what happened with Denise and I. Denise left her *first love* – who was *God* – for a life with me. After all, she had free will to exercise her rights even at that young age. The problem was, I didn't know God, so how could I adequately lead her in righteousness? As a result, Denise and I would have to endure living a life without the true God until He came to reclaim us.

Though only 14, it didn't take long before we had fallen deeply in love. I was one of the captains of our high school football team and Denise was running for office as class secretary. I remember thinking that I wanted to be with her for the rest of my life. I don't know why I thought that at the time. Of course, she was beautiful and intelligent, but we were both first loves and I knew nothing about girls.

My only other interests were sports and working out. Those were my passions. Yet here I was totally taken by this girl at the young age of 14.

Although I was an honor student throughout high school, I had no aspirations to do anything special after high school except work, in order to earn money. I lived in Stateway Gardens, which was a large housing complex consisting of several 17 story project buildings, lined up side by side, also situated on the city's south side. In the early years the area was clean and safe. But as the years passed, Stateway Gardens came to be crime ridden, and had the reputation of one of the most dangerous places to live in Chicago. Even most Chicago police officers feared entering the neighborhood.

It became commonplace for officers entering that area to be showered with pop bottles and dangerous debris being thrown down upon them from lookouts atop the buildings. There were an estimated 1,000-2,000 plus underprivileged people packed on top of one other amid 17 floors in each project building, with at least 6-8 buildings in a row reaching up into the city's landscape.

Obviously, many families lived as victims in their own neighborhood. Several well-connected street gangs were spawned from these projects and typically ran the neighborhood.

I remember one major gang had initiated a draft. A draft operated like this: if you were a young teenaged male who lived in the project area, you would be approached by several gang members who would inform you that you were being drafted into their gang. You were then given a time and a location of a gang meeting, whereupon you would report and then be initiated into the gang. If one valued his future and more importantly, his life, one showed up at the meeting. With at least six to eight families housed on each floor of each project building, and each family having several children, there was a surplus of future gang members from which to choose. There were three major gangs operating in the area including The Blackstone Rangers (later called the Black P-Stone Nation), The Black-Gangster Disciples, and The Vicelords. At one time there were said to be

13,000 Blackstone Rangers…a membership that exceeded the entire Chicago Police Dept.

Though as a child growing up, even in the middle of all the violence, it was simply home to me. That large an amount of people packed in a small radius of real estate space was a city within itself. Since we were poor, I always felt I needed to get out and make money as soon as possible in order to help support my family. As an African American teenager back in those days, the thought of spending another 4-8 years in college seemed like an eternity, and the long way to achieve success and financial freedom. When your family comes from extremely meager beginnings, the need of finding steady work and trying to make it without becoming dependent on public assistance can prove to be quite a challenge. The drive to attain money at any cost can cause one to lack the vision needed to reach for higher goals in life. Worse still, some succumbed to their plight, and resorted to violence and illegal activity in an attempt to secure a foothold in life.

Miraculously, I wasn't lured in that direction. Surely I lived in the midst of chaos. Many of my closest friends gambled, dealt drugs, and some even wound up dead, while still others were convicted of murder themselves. Good young men were lost and swallowed up by sin and poverty. But God knew me long before I knew Him. And He insulated me. As you will see, God kept both my wife and me. Just as the bible says in Psalms 91,

"A thousand may fall at your side, and ten thousand at your right hand; But it shall not come near you."

I was an athlete and I excelled in school, even though my school district was lacking in resources. The more advanced academic programs and curriculums that were afforded to children attending suburban and private schools were not available in the school district where Denise and I lived. Although I did well as an honor student in my high school, our school's overall scholastic achievements were probably only slightly above average in comparison to private and/or more progressive

11

schools. There wasn't an urgent push in guiding inner city children in my area to levels of higher education; therefore, like many inner city youngsters, I dreamt of either becoming a professional football player or some other type of sports star. This seemed to be the quickest route to achieving what I felt I needed in life.

Of course, I now know different since the Lord came to me. Since meeting Jesus, I have received such an awakening in every area of my life. I can now impart this valuable information to other adults as well as young people who may feel trapped in hopeless situations. Such is the liberty one receives when one enters into a true relationship with the Creator, who is Christ Jesus.

But back then I did not know the Lord, and had no inclination to follow the Christian faith. As a matter of fact, Christianity seemed like a big joke to me. From birth to the age of 49, I had never been to a church service in my life. I had never even read one single bible scripture. I reasoned, "Why should I? That stuff isn't true at all." Funny, although I didn't believe in Christianity at all, as I grew older and became an upperclassman in high school, I also wasn't sold on my family's religion of Islam. I've always been one to think, "If it sounds too good to be true, it probably is." Needless to say, from what I had heard, there were just too many gaps in both Christianity as well as the doctrine expounded by the Nation of Islam.

While most so-called Christians I knew seemed to be hypocrites, *hearers but not doers of the word,* some things I would hear my parents say concerning their group's Islamic doctrine just didn't make sense to me either. It seemed to be mostly folklore and tradition. No matter how passionate one felt about either...I would need definite proof if I were to follow at all. I would later learn that following religion and following Jesus are two entirely different things. Many people in the church are full when it comes to religiosity, but running on empty when it comes to truly having Jesus in their gas tank. The bible tells us in James 2:20 that *faith without works is dead.* If Christians are truly living Christ centered lives it will show up in their day-to-day conduct.

But growing up, I saw these people who professed to be Christians, cursing, stealing, carousing, fornicating, etc. My parents told me that being a Christian was not the way to go, and I believed that. But as I said earlier, I wasn't sold on their "religion," either. Surely there were some of the same sinful acts that I saw in Christians being committed in the people of my parent's religious doctrine. But out of fear and respect for my parents, I never questioned them about their faith. I just decided to be thankful that they didn't force their religion on me.

CHAPTER TWO

TAKE NO PRISONERS

By the time Denise and I became seniors in high school, I had at least 12 major college university football scholarship offers. I had been blessed to be strong and athletic and had my choice of schools ranging from Dartmouth College to Purdue University, with various small colleges in between. I first accepted a four year football scholarship to Boise State College simply because it was the Alma Mater of one of my high school coaches. I reported early in the summer of 1973. At that time, the only students on campus were a few other incoming scholarship athletes. I had never been outside of Chicago in my life. For me, a city boy from the projects of Chicago to be transplanted in a rural town, given a job and a bicycle to ride five miles to and from work proved to be a bit much. Racism was a culture shock, and I decided to leave Boise Idaho.

I was truly dismayed and quickly became homesick and finally dropped out of school. I also admit that a large part of my decision to leave school was because I missed Denise, who was still in Chicago at the time. I also lacked patience and needed money. Against the advice of the coaching staff, I left Boise and headed back home to Chicago. That same week, I opted to join the military in an effort to begin earning money and get a foothold in life.

At the time, the Army recruiters promised that the military would provide me with valuable job training and a few hundred dollars a month. In those days $400 a month was pretty good money for an 18-year-old. I reasoned that I could save a little money each month as a small nest egg for Denise and me until I was done in the military.

While I was home on leave, Denise and I went to the justice of the peace and were married. We celebrated by enjoying a delicious *Dagwood Burger* (which was a huge triple-decker burger big enough for two people; it came with cheese, onions, mushrooms...the works) at a little old fashioned restaurant called Flo's in downtown Chicago.

I believe that burger was named after Dagwood, (the husband of the character in the movie *Blondie*). I shudder now as I carefully monitor my cholesterol levels thinking, "Wow, did we really used to eat like that?"

Soon after, I was sent to Korea and served on the Demilitarized Zone near the border of North Korea. There were skirmishes and periodic military engagements occurring along the DMZ, and it was during this time that I realized that my life could be in jeopardy. I feared that I might be killed while serving on the border of these two warring countries (North and South Korea). Still I had taken it upon myself to enlist. So although it had not been my intention to serve in Korea when I had originally signed up in the military, I couldn't blame anyone except myself.

I had been careful to sign a "guaranteed contract" upon enlisting in the Army. That contract supposedly guaranteed that I would serve in Europe upon completing my basic and MOS (Military Occupational Specialty) training.

A relative of mine had enlisted about one year prior to my joining the service and he was stationed in Europe and loving every minute of it.

The ability to travel to Europe was also one of the reasons I had joined the service. So to be sent to Korea where there was still isolated violence and a civil war separating the country was not what I had in mind. Somehow there had been a glitch in the system and *Uncle Sam* shipped me out to Korea. So, I looked into getting reassigned to Europe. The military accepted my reassignment request, promising to correct the error. However, in the meantime you can guess where I was to be found; that's right, the DMZ on the border of North Korea.

I decided to immerse myself in training earnestly in martial arts and survival techniques: lifting weights and running 5 miles per day through the hills amidst the rice patties. Ironically, I would never *truly* learn about *real* survival techniques until nearly 38 years later when Jesus came into my life. I often explain to people that God only allowed me to learn physical and mental survival training in order to grasp the concepts needed to *transition* into *spiritual* survival training.

During my time in the military, Denise moved in with my family. She had no conflicts with my parents or their choice of religion. My mother and Denise bonded instantly; my mother loved her as if she were her own. Fact is, my mother actually came to be closer to Denise than she was to her own daughters. Such was the strength of their mother and daughter bond.

It was during that time that Denise began adopting some of the customs of my parents' religion such as not eating pork and refraining from consuming tobacco and alcohol. Again, God was at work even then because although my parents were not in Christ, God took the best of what they practiced (which was love and unity in a secure family structure) and allowed those things to work for Denise's benefit.

After my short stint in the military, I received an honorable discharge. I was picked up on a full football scholarship at Drake University, in Des Moines, IA and jumped at the opportunity to resume my collegiate football career. I was nearing 20 years of age at the time. Denise and I headed out to Drake University in Iowa. The military had taught me a thing or two about making hasty decisions, but still I had blinders on which caused me to sometimes jump the gun.

So elated was I to be finished with the military, that I signed a letter of intent to Drake University, passing up a football scholarship offer at Purdue University simply because Purdue couldn't sign me until the following semester.

The ironic part was that Purdue was known for its boilermaker football teams, while the Drake Bulldogs were known for track and basketball. In retrospect, it probably would have served my football interests better to wait out the 3-4 months required in order to attend Purdue, especially since my high school had already sent one outstanding athlete to Purdue the year before I graduated. It would have been wonderful to compete at Purdue with such a close friend.

I now know that wasn't God's plan for me. But back then at my age during that time of my life, I didn't have a clue.

I decided to truly focus on preparing to play in the National Football League. I was always a big, strong young man, and football came easy for me. I had been an All State linebacker in high school football. I was considered by many to be a potential pro football prospect. I had size and intelligence, and something that may be even more important if one is expected to make it as a professional linebacker in football. I had a seething competitive rage within me.

I was always eager to go into battle on the field and take no prisoners. The late football coach of Florida A&M University, Jake Gaither, coined a phrase years ago when he said, "I like my boys agile, mobile and hostile." Truly, I was all those things.

At times I was held out of practice by my coaches for fear that I would put our team at a disadvantage by injuring one of our players prior to a game -- not through dirty tactics, but because of sheer aggressiveness. I would learn later that God would channel that aggressive style in a heavenly direction.

CHAPTER THREE

IN FULL SWING

I continued to excel in football at Drake where I was served as captain and was selected as an All-Conference athlete, gaining some notoriety in newspapers and major college sports magazines. I was pretty sure that I would wind up playing somewhere in the NFL. I was ultimately contacted by an agent and was scouted by pro teams. It looked as though things would turn out just as I expected; I would be selected by an NFL team and finally be able to support Denise and our families in the proper manner. But to my dismay, my knee was injured at the beginning of my senior year in college.

I then had to try out as a free agent at a Dallas Cowboys minicamp and eventually signed with the USFL's Arizona Wranglers. The knee injury, though not considered career ending, was just enough to keep me from performing at my optimum level. And I must say this to all of our young athletes still aspiring to someday play at the professional level. You can have all of the physical and mental ingredients needed to make it in the pros, but all it takes is one injury to derail your career. So never put all of your hope in sports. Instead put it in God and ask Him to guide you in both your academic and sports career.

Due to my nagging injury I found myself unable to sustain the momentum needed to make it through a football season at my former physical level. At one time it looked as if I had a good shot at the pros, but after the lingering knee injury I was left disappointed and dismayed. Eventually I stopped chasing the dream of football. My wife and I headed to California as a young couple looking to find our place in the world. While the dream of playing pro football was fading from my system, I began to focus on making a living in the Bay Area. A friend of mine talked me into applying for a job as a police officer. I was soon hired and served on a large police department in the Bay Area. By this time we had a 5-year-old son. And at that point, Denise and I began raising our nuclear family. Denise gave birth to our second child, a baby girl in 1983. Our family life was now in full swing. I was the main breadwinner in the family, while Denise worked part time and attended school, as well as raised the children.

My wife and I both loved to sing and had been singing on and off as a duet in college. Denise had an incredible singing voice and was a very accomplished theater actress as well. I had been fortunate enough at the time to become a member with the Screen Actor's Guild and earn roles in a couple of movies and commercials. I landed a couple of commercials, one was a yellow pages ad that nearly went national titled *Fuzzy*, in which I played the part of –you guessed it–a football player. That part landed me a speaking role, which opened the door to a larger role in a movie of the week titled, *The King of Love*. Now don't get the wrong idea, the film was nothing like the title implies. I played the role of a radical revolutionary nicknamed *Blue*. I had one speaking role in this movie, but was seen throughout the film. The climactic end of the movie was a dramatic shooting scene where I engaged the FBI in a shootout, and of course was killed. This TV movie of the week brought more auditions and the acting agency to which I belonged suggested that I should move down to Los Angeles.

There I would be housed in an apartment with other actors and do nothing but make auditions daily. At that time –during the late 80's and 90's–most of the major roles were handed out in Southern California. In order for me to take advantage of this career move would mean leaving my family for a time, to pursue acting full time. However, I couldn't see leaving my family. I decided to remain in the Bay Area of northern California. I was soon awarded a nice role in the *Midnight Caller* TV series, which was being filmed in Oakland, California. The episode was called *Take Back the Streets.* Actors Dan Mancusso and Mykel T. Williamson starred in it, and I was cast as a street thug named *Buddha.* I was now beginning to receive larger roles on TV. I was also striking up friendships with well respected and accomplished actors and actresses such as the late Theodore Wilson of *That's My Mama,* and Madge Sinclair of *Trapper John MD* fame. Although Denise was

26

not with the Screen Actor's Guild, she was a most accomplished and talented theater actress. However, it was much more difficult for a female to break into the business than a male. So our lives revolved around me working as an officer to support the family and Denise and me making auditions, acting, and singing in our private time. I would pick up parts as best I could, and collect royalties. On the weekends we found enjoyment singing and doing deejay work in clubs in the Bay Area of Northern California. We were regulars in many of the R&B venues in the Bay Area, performing at *Kimball's East,* which was a well-known supper club in the Bay Area, as well as singing at the Monterey Blues Festival in Monterey, California. As we began to gain notoriety acting and singing, Denise and I started planning to make a living with our music and possibly sing overseas. Since we loved to sing and perform, we thought, "What better way to work than doing something we love?" We knew that we could sing together as a duet and did not have to audition. Therefore, we immersed ourselves into the music. We were interested in doing all things musical. We performed with bands, worked as deejays, sang at

27

weddings, anniversaries, New Year's Eve parties and events, nightclubs, as well as Karaoke clubs and functions. So from about 1984 to 2004, Denise and I did the music routine, performing with various Bay Area artists. We were known as *Dee & Jay*. We felt that we were getting closer to reaching our dream and the security that our talents would bring. So far, I had been extremely good at sports…but it didn't work out due to injuries, but we were both good at singing and acting. Denise had been a finalist years ago in the audition for original cast of the *Dreamgirls* musical. But neither of us was willing to go to Hollywood and uproot our somewhat secure family lifestyle in northern California. Ah, but singing and traveling together….that, we could do. After all, both our children had now graduated from high school, with our son beginning his career and our daughter beginning junior college. Little did we know that God had other plans for us, BIG plans, *Plans to give us a future and a hope* (Jeremiah 29:11), not in entertaining, but in serving Him.

CHAPTER FOUR

SQUEALING LIKE A CHILD

It was in the late summer August of 2004, a few days after my 49th birthday that our lives would change forever. That year all of our previous plans came to a screeching halt. Our very existence took an entirely different direction. It was a balmy summer evening. My wife and I were performing at *Kimball's East*. We happened to be singing with a group called the *Motown Revue*. The revue consisted of several vocal artists and musicians who would pay tribute to the music of the famed Motown era. Denise and I headlined, performing the music of the *Ike & Tina Turner Revue*. It was a very popular musical revue, full of nostalgia, excitement, and secular R&B music.

That evening we finished a late night gig and by the time the singers and dancers piled out to go home, it was about 12:30AM. I had just slid into the driver's seat of our modest 2002 Toyota Corolla. I was waiting for Denise to exit the club. Typically, she would be one of the last performers to leave the club. No matter how exhausting the set was, my wife always seemed to find the energy to spend extra time hugging and kissing the other artists and fans as if it was goodbye forever. I didn't understand it at the time, but I now realize that just as a TV set that is bought cable compatible, is designed and prepared to receive not just the regular four channels, but numerous channels including HBO, Showtime, On Demand, etc., God had designed Denise with a deep love for people, ready to be connected to His signal. She had a genuine love for people, even strangers. She just wasn't hooked up to God. But that was about to change.

As I waited in the car, I heard Denise's very distinct musical voice exclaiming, "Oh they're so beautiful…Oh my goodness, so beautiful!" At the time, I was parked in the parking lot with the rear of our car facing toward the dressing room door of the club, so I couldn't see my wife's face. I could only hear her voice, so I just figured that her excitement was the result of her and the girls in the revue viewing outfits or pictures in a photo album or something as they walked to their cars. I remember thinking, "It's 12:30AM, I'm sweaty and tired...I'm ready to go home, I wish she'd hurry." Soon Denise reached the car and got in. I looked at her and saw that her eyes were wide with wonder. She hopped into the front passenger seat next to me, and stared out of the window, not even turning in my direction...still excitedly saying, "Oh my, what beautiful colors." It was then that I realized that she hadn't been speaking to our fellow cast members. She appeared to be describing colors that she was seeing. Problem was, I didn't see them. So I of course said, "Honey, what are you talking about... what colors?" She didn't even look my way. Her eyes continued to focus in front of her and she gasped while smiling in awe "Don't you see them Joel, they're all around us...they're so beautiful." I had started the car and we were now driving out of the lot to Powell Street, and heading toward the I-80 East freeway in the Bay Area.

I tried to come to some reasonable explanation as to why she was seeing colors. I said, "Dear, it's dark, it's 12:30AM. There are no colors in the sky." She dismissed my remark. Shaking her head convincingly, she said,

"No, I see them. They're beautiful." I frantically searched my mind for a reason, an explanation as to what was going on with my wife. Then it came to me. Of course, we had been singing and dancing, performing for nearly three hours nonstop. We had been sweating under the hot stage lights, and just like when one is working out, the sweat at times finds its way into the eyes. I recalled that several times after enduring heavy workout sessions, even after showering, that when I focused my eyes on a light such as a streetlight, I would see a slight halo. Whew, was I glad. I told her, "Girl, what you must be seeing is a halo because of the sweat that must have seeped into your eyes."

"No!!" she said loudly, cutting me off in mid-sentence; "They're all around, they're on the headlights, the streetlights the stoplights...they're red and yellow blue, and purple and green...they're so beautiful, Joel, and they're everywhere." The words tumbled out of her mouth. I was becoming nervous, not knowing what to make of my wife's behavior. She continued squealing like a child. Whatever she was experiencing was so bright and beautiful that she was completely captivated for the 20 minutes or so that it took for me to drive us home. I don't even remember Denise ever once focusing her eyes on me the entire time it took for us to reach our house. As we exited the car and walked to our front door, she was still looking upward and left to right, gasping delightfully as if surrounded by these rainbow colored halos. Frantic with concern, I fought to keep calm and not upset her. I was desperately trying to make sense of what was happening. As we entered the house, I quietly began putting away our costumes, guitar, and supplies. Denise was in the rear of the house. Eventually I nervously called her to the front door and asked her to take a look outside and tell me if she still saw the colors. She excitedly came forward smiling, but as she looked out, her smile slowly faded, replaced by a frown.

Dejectedly she said, "No…they're gone." I was so relieved. I suggested she get some sleep. It had been a long day. I tucked her into bed. As she curled under the covers, I watched her fall asleep. As she closed her eyes I heard her sigh, "They were so… beautiful," and she

33

drifted off to sleep. Unfortunately, I couldn't sleep. I was worried nearly out of my mind. I wondered why this happened. Why was my wife seeing things? Neither of us smoked, drank, or did drugs of any kind. Heck, we didn't even drink coffee. The strongest thing we would consume was probably soft drinks/soda pop on occasion. I was left searching for a reason that would explain why this incident had occurred. As Denise slept, I paced the floor, suddenly remembering that I seemed to recall reading someplace that there was a person who either had a brain tumor or was going blind and he had seen flashes of colors or something like that.

"Oh, no!" I thought, "Maybe she's got some dreadful problem with her eyes or her brain!" I decided to take her in for an exam, but it would have to wait until morning. I can't recall how long I slept, if at all. But the next day, I was up bright and early. I remember saying to Denise, as nonchalant as I could, "Hey…what do you say we go and get an eye examination today?" She quickly complied, and off we went to the doctor's office. She passed with flying colors. I took another step and had an overall checkup, and she passed that as well.

After Denise was given a clean bill of health, an onsite nurse told her, "I'm glad everything checked out, because when you came into our office you had an aura around you." I didn't understand what this woman meant by that, but I was just glad Denise had received a clean bill of health, both mentally and physically. Yet and still, I wasn't at peace with what had occurred. But as the days went by, I figured, "Oh well, she was probably just exhausted, it's over and we will just move on." I had no idea what would happen next. No more than a few days after Denise had seen the rainbow-like colors, we encountered another situation that was even more puzzling and troubling than the first. I was at home with my wife when I noticed her right index finger twitching and moving as if she were using it to write. At the time, she appeared to be writing on her thigh. She was engrossed in the moving of her finger, seemingly impervious to me. After watching her for a few seconds, I asked her, "Umm, what are you doing?" She looked up at me briefly, and said, "I can read this." She then looked back down as her finger, and continued to scrawl along her upper leg.

Refusing to just let this go by, I looked at her and said matter-of-factly, "What do you mean you can read this? You're moving your finger yourself." "No!!" she said loudly, not even bothering to look up at me, "Joel I'm not moving it, it's moving by itself." Before I could object further, she exclaimed, looking intently in the direction of her finger as if reading a message, "They're saying that they are angels and God has a plan for us." Immediately several waves of emotion swept over me. I was beset with fear, anger, exasperation, defiance, helplessness and curiosity, all at the same time. In desperation I raised my voice at her saying, "What do you mean, they're saying they're angels?" I was afraid and I was desperate. The only reply I was willing to accept was that this was not happening. I wanted Denise to tell me that she was joking. Not waiting for her to even answer me, I said, "Don't tell me that! You are moving your finger!" Pleading with Denise I said, "C'mon, don't tell

36

me that." But my wife looked at me with fear and bewilderment in her eyes. Tearfully, quietly, she said, "That's what the writing said." I tried to gather myself, and thought for a moment, not wanting to explode. I then said to her, "The next time this happens, grab an ink pen, rest your hand on a piece of paper and let it go. That way I can read what is going on, and see what this is all about." Denise slowly nodded her head saying okay.

I didn't have to wait much longer for this to occur again. Less than two days later, Denise's finger began moving. She retrieved a sheet of paper and for all intents and purposes appeared to be a secretary taking a shorthand dictation of some sort. She began reading slowly and carefully as she wrote, deciphering the message so that I could hear. The message did indeed say that they were angels. They instructed us to be good, and not to dance too provocatively when performing. They told Denise not to wear her skirts too short or kick her legs too high. They ended the message by telling Denise and me that God has a plan for us and that Jesus would visit us soon. How's that for letting your fingers do the talking?

CHAPTER FIVE

EVERY MAN FOR HIMSELF

I was left shaken and confused, for many obvious reasons. Of course our act at the time included many of Tina Turner's routines, with the finale being the hit tune, *Rolling on the River*. Between Denise's singing and sashaying across the stage, playing the role of Tina, and all of the other female dancers, there were plenty of short skirts and lots of high kicking going on. But what was even more troubling to me was that I had spent my entire life completely disregarding the notion that the Christian faith might possibly be viable or true.

Because I didn't know God or truly believe in Jesus, I felt I had to make my way through this world as best I could. What else could I do? It was every man for himself. Take care of your family and yourself the best way you know how. Of course, by adopting that pre-conceived mindset, I was left with miles of room for error. I reasoned in my mind that if I made mistakes it was okay. After all, I rationalized that I was basically a good man, taking care of my family to the best of my ability. Sure, I had secret sins that I didn't want her to find out about, especially my unfaithfulness to her. At the time I reasoned within myself to justify my actions. I began to believe the lie that I created that all men cheated, and I was afraid that Denise would learn of my adulterous ways. My mind raced at the thought of what would happen when the truth came out through these angels, if they were indeed angels, and if Jesus was real!

I wondered, *"Why is this happening to Denise and me?* So although I was stymied as to what in the world was going on, I was fairly certain that Denise was not pulling my leg. I had known her practically all of my life, and a more honest, practical and down to earth human being could not be found, of this I was convinced. She has never been motivated by greed, sensationalism, etc. She was not a diva, not one to be easily taken away by dramatics, nor by her imagination. So there were only two other reasons this could be happening. Either 1) this was absolutely true, or 2) my wife was seriously sick. I had to place myself in a very precarious neutral position.

You see, although I wasn't ready for this, I wanted this to be true, if only to be assured that my wife was okay health wise. However, the flip side of this is that I wasn't completely ready to find out if Christianity was true, because that meant that my parents had spent their entire lives serving something that was false. It also meant that I had been absolutely incorrect in assuming that Jesus was just a fictional character or at most, just a prophet and a good man with good intentions. But the most unnerving thing was that if this was true, I had lived my entire life of 49 years as a total sinner, apart from God. And the sad part of it was that during those 49 years I loved sinning and wondered, even as I was pondering the validity of Denise's divine writing, how I could keep my sins hidden. I'm ashamed to admit it, but it's true. Since my conversion to Christ I now know that, *"Each one is tempted when he is drawn away by his own desires and enticed. Then, when desire has conceived, it gives birth to sin"* (as it says in James 1: 14-15a.).

Now you're probably wondering just what sins I had been harboring. Aside from being a liar and a cheat,

I had a temper that was extremely destructive. My coaches say I was voted the meanest player ever to play for my high school football team. My ex-coach once said, "Joel, you could start a fight in a room by yourself." Of course, that is not quite accurate. I usually appeared calm and reserved, but I could easily explode when provoked. It was my controlled rage and fearlessness that made me a valued linebacker. It was that ferocious attitude that made me a champion martial artist and fighter. These skills made performing my duties in police work easy as well, where I was usually one of the first at the scene of a shooting or the first to go through the door of a dangerous situation. But it was that same warrior mentality that the devil used to fuel my sins of the flesh, which led to my being unfaithful as a husband.

You see, growing in a survival of the fittest environment, I had adopted a death wish mentality of sorts. Now I do not mean that I wanted to die. But when it came to competing in violent contact sports such as football, boxing, and martial arts, one's physical prowess was paramount if one was to ever aspire to compete at a professional or championship level. You knew that each time you entered a stadium or a fighter's ring someone would win and someone had to lose...the winner takes all. There is much sacrifice with training, so athletes will typically freely accept the fringe benefits received from pleasure that arises from living dangerous lives associated with pain. This same mentality is even more prevalent in police work, where hazardous and potentially fatal duty assignments come daily. It comes with the territory. Officers typically know that each day you wear your uniform, or strap on your weapon, it could be your last. Therefore, you tend to live each day as if it were your last. I realized that the work that I was involved in could bring death at any time. That being said, the temptations posed by the opposite sex many times were met with acceptance, spoils of war so to speak. Whether they're called groupies in sports, or beat wives in law enforcement (women who make themselves available to officers on their assigned beats), they weren't difficult to find.

These casual encounters that peppered my past had been viewed as incidental contact (minor incidences of contact likely to result due to the harsh realities of my work). I had come to actually believe that my infidelity wasn't harmful as long as it remained hidden and somewhat innocuous. I saw no reason why my sins would ever be called to the forefront. But somehow, even with my limited understanding of the things of the Spirit, my past escapades now felt burdensome. For if they were seen in the Spirit, would the results be manifested in the physical?

These resulting sins were now of great concern to me. I knew that if my indiscretions were revealed, they could destroy my marriage and cause my wife to leave me. And although I hid behind the excuse of not knowing God, I now realize that all of God's creation has knowledge of Him,

"For since the creation of the world His invisible attributes are clearly seen, being understood by the things that are made, even His eternal power and

Godhead, so that they are without excuse." (Romans 1:20)

"Are they not all ministering spirits sent forth to minister for those who will inherit salvation?" (Hebrews 1:14)

So during the times that my wife first started receiving these messages, I was being prepared in my mind for the amazing work that God had put into play for our lives.

I can't recall how many of these supernatural messages Denise and I received within the next few days, but approximately 4-5 days later I came home from work pretty tired and was met by my very excited wife. She greeted me grinning, saying,

"Hi honey, look what the angels sent us."

She was holding a note pad and was about to read the message to me, when I abruptly stuck my hand out as if I were a crossing guard,

"Stop!" I said, in a loud voice. Look, I don't want to hear about any angels today...I'm tired...and I don't want to hear it, okay? Anyway, if they really are angels, and if they love us so much, ask them what the lottery numbers are for this week."

As I sit here now, 8 years later, I still shake my head in disbelief at how blind and ignorant I was. To think that at one time in my life I was foolish enough to actually have the audacity to attempt to place an order to God's holy angels for money as if I were at a take-out deli, ordering a sandwich to go (such was the magnitude of my ignorance).

After hearing my ridiculous request, Denise looked at me with her mouth open. Suddenly her hand started moving, and she began feverishly scrawling a message on her pad. As Denise wrote, she began reading aloud, slowly and clearly, the following words,

"Joel, Joel, Joel, We don't give lottery numbers! But aren't you already wealthy?

Don't you have good health? Don't you have a good job, a nice home? Don't you have a beautiful wife and two beautiful, intelligent children?"

I was completely disarmed. I didn't know what to say. I stood there dumbfounded, and found myself regretting I had ever asked that stupid question about lottery numbers in the first place. It wasn't that I didn't already know how fortunate I was to have such good health, a wonderful family, and a good job. With all that was presently going on in our lives, I was just so frustrated for answers. I wasn't much of a gambler, but occasionally when the lottery jackpot was over a million dollars I would play a few numbers, most times not over $5.00. And although I did believe there was something going on with my wife and these angels, I couldn't exactly say that I was completely sold.

So, being an uninformed sinner, I had in effect, irreverently requested that the angels reveal the winning lottery numbers as a way of proving to me their true existence. At the time I just figured ... "What if?" I remember hearing someone once saying, "You miss every shot that you don't take."

But of course, I now know God, and I know He is omniscient and knows all things. Therefore, if God sends you ministering spirits to get your attention, it will be for God's purpose and plan for your life, not your will. Hallelujah to Jesus!

So, after the angels had reminded me to take stock of what I already had, Denise's hand continued to write; and she continued reading the words, slowly and clearly. The next words the angels said served to quickly leap over my ever-shortening wall of doubt, and reverberate in my ears as Denise read aloud, "We know you believe us a little Joel…but how would you like to see us?" Just for a few seconds…I couldn't speak.

That question had caught me completely off guard. Denise on the other hand, could speak. And she wasted no time, throwing her ink pen to the ground and backing away, screaming in fear, "No…I don't want to see you!!" For a moment there was silence. But that brief span of time, which I figured was precipitated by Denise's refusal of the angel's offer, gave me the opportunity to recover from my stupor. As if answering involuntarily, I managed to blurt out, "Yes," as I nodded my head, "I would like to see you." Denise's hand had stopped moving because the angels had ceased speaking until I had offered an answer to their question. I told Denise to pick up the pen. I knew she was afraid... and I admit, I was a little scared as well, but I was at a crossroad. Nonetheless, I believed that she did not doubt that she was receiving messages from these angels, but the cop in me needed evidence, direct evidence. Denise picked up the pen. I could plainly see the fear that was on her face as her hand began scribbling. Denise's voice was now shaking slightly as she gathered herself.

Looking intently at the writing produced by divine power from God on high through His angels, these words came forth,

"We knew Denise would not want to see us, for she would be afraid if she saw anything in this house. But

49

we think you can handle it, Joel. We will soon pay you a visit. You'll know us when you see us."

The writing then stopped. Denise slowly looked up at me, still astonished and terrified at the thought of what had just been said. I stood there looking in my wife's direction. Nodding my head, my voice was quietly saying, "Okay...okay."

I spent the next few days in a fog, anxiously wondering how these angels would show themselves to me. One part of me wanted to believe totally in them and their claim that God had a plan for my wife and me. I was desperate for a tangible answer to the question of why all these things had recently began to happen in the lives of my wife and me. Why us...why now? After all, I had no real problems with my life up to that particular time, other than the things most people have to go through; like having to pay bills, keeping the phone and electricity turned on, etc. I felt that by stepping up to accept this offer to see these angels, this whole episode would somehow blow over and just go away, and Denise and I could move on, putting this peculiar chapter of our lives to rest.

It was about a week and a few days later, and I'd not seen any angels cross my path. I was slowly beginning to resign myself to the fact that this whole thing had been just a slight interruption in the lives of Denise and I, and things would now return to normal. I remember thinking that I would be okay with that. No real harm, therefore, no real foul as the old saying goes. I remember thinking that whatever was going on with Denise and this divine writing thing, could be worked out.

Denise would later tell me that these messages, when received from the angels, entered her and went from her heart, to her hand. In my mind I reasoned that whatever the case may be, I would have to deal with it as best I could, even if it were to turn out that although she believed it, it was all in her mind, like the story of *A Beautiful Mind.*

Inwardly I recalled an old comedy TV show called *Harvey the Six Foot Rabbit,* about a man who insisted that he had a friend who was a 6 ft. tall rabbit named *Harvey*, and although no one believed him, this man was allowed to communicate with this invisible 6 ft. tall rabbit.

"That's right," I thought, "Denise's situation is similar in that she is communicating with invisible angels and isn't threatening to harm herself or anyone else. So whatever is going on with her is fine. I love her and will never leave her, even if it turns out that she winds up needing mental help after all." Boy was I in for a surprise.

"But as it is written: "Eye has not seen, nor ear heard, nor have entered into the heart of man the things which God has prepared for those who love Him." (1 Corinthians 2:9)

CHAPTER SIX

DANGER, TROUBLE, AND ME

During that time in late 2004 and early 2005, I was on a strict physical training regimen. I said in the beginning of this testimony that I had always been interested in training and fitness. I used to get out of bed faithfully at 3:00AM and dress in sweats, leaving my house en route to the gymnasium. Although this took discipline, I found it easier to get up early and train before going to work, rather than attempting to get it done after work.

There was something about the peace and serenity of rising early in the morning while most people were still asleep that gave me a sense of accomplishment. Back then, rising early and engaging in a heart thumping working routine was my stabilizer, my private time. My early morning workouts were like exhaust valves blowing out any residual stress my body and mind might secretly be holding on to. In police work, dealing with the criminal element daily has a tendency to wear on one physically as well as mentally, especially if one does not know the Lord.

In those days, without Jesus in my life, I was desperately seeking to keep things together myself. I was regarded as a problem solver, for the public's safety, as well as for my own personal problems. As if that were not enough, many of my friends, even officers who knew of my "all the way, first through the door mentality," would bring their problems to me. Although I never sought to gain this type of notoriety from friends and the public, it certainly seemed to follow me. One citizen and her son often addressed me as *Robocop*. I was in popular demand for everything from fixing people's ticket problems to dealing with armed suspects both on and off duty.

Not to feel sorry for myself, but to all of our fellow law enforcement heroes striving to do all they can to serve and protect the public; if you don't know Jesus, who protects the protector, if only from himself?

It seems a paradox, but I came to really look forward to gaining relief from the past day's stressful events by enduring a grueling 2-2 1/2 hr work out, then cooling down before I faced the new day. There were times when I would workout even twice in the same day, running and lifting for hours in the morning then sparring in the evenings for another 2-21/2 hrs. I felt I had to stay able and ready to handle whatever might come. I now know that the devil is very sly and will even use the very things that you are good at, and constantly supply them to you, in order to allow you to overdo things. Here I was, a non-smoker, non-drinker, non-drug user, yet I was hooked just the same. It was just another form of addiction. I was addicted to danger, fueled by pride, paranoia, and what I considered preparation. And although I never looked for trouble, I never thought about running away from it either, therefore, it always found me. We met in the strangest places, danger, trouble, and me. I was no more than a mouse in a cylinder running through my workouts, yet running with Satan, and repeating the course daily.

Anyway, this particular day started no differently. I awoke and walked into the restroom to wash up. As I turned on the faucet, I looked into the mirror facing me. I noticed what appeared to be vertical static lines vibrating on the wall. These lines resembled the static seen back in the days when you would turn on an old black and white TV set. These lines seemed to be vibrating, as if taking shape.

Initially I thought I had double vision (since I had just awakened), so I rubbed my eyes in an effort to regain my normal eyesight. But as I looked again, now staring intently in the mirror, I clearly saw that the lines were taking on distinct shapes. The shapes were in the form of human bodies. There were three sets of lines forming into three distinct human figures. I squinted, and bucked my eyes, wondering just what was going on. The bathroom was beginning to fog up due to the hot water running, so... keeping my eyes on these shapes, I slowly and carefully turned off the faucet. The forms continued to come into view. They were slightly transparent. I noticed that I could see through them to the walls that were behind them. Still, I could see them clearly. They were translucent, meaning that they seemed to blend in with the color of my bathroom walls and cabinets. Still, I tried to block them out. I remember turning quickly to my left averting my eyes away from them, but they were there. Instantly I turned to the right…but they were there as well, whichever way I looked… I gasped, thinking, *"I can't get away from them…but I must."* I was desperate to prove that this was not happening.

"This can't be happening," I thought.

I was determined to prove them wrong. I had to. I felt I had to save my wife, our relationship, and our stability. Our very lives as we had come to know them depended upon this nightmare going away once and for all. Yet, I couldn't escape the images of these three angels staring me down. I began feeling something that was normally foreign to me. It was fear. Fear was now taking hold of me, yet I tried to fight it off. I defiantly shut my eyes as tightly as I could.

Whimpering, I thought to myself, *"Whatever this is, whatever is going on, whoever you are, I am not going to look at you ...I refuse!"*

But as I closed my eyes in an effort not to see them, there they were, as bold as ever. In the darkness, with my eyes being closed, I now saw them even better than with my eyes open. They were now bright white and fully formed. It was as if the background of the blackness highlighted the angels. Quietly, in submission to this reality, I began to cry.

Here I was, a 49-year-old, veteran police sergeant, a man who had seen so much violence, so much death and destruction that I was practically immune to sorrow and fear. I even remember not being able to cry at my mother's funeral because I had seen so much sadness in my life. Yet here I was, shaking, murmuring incoherently. I could not move from that spot. I could see these three beings staring not just at me, but into me. Each of these angels had the form of human beings, no wings. Each was positioned differently. The angel on the left had his hands at his side. The angel on the opposite end had his hands on his hips. The one in the middle held his opposite elbow in the palm of his opposite hand, while his other hand supported his chin. He was leaning forward toward me as if examining me. His stare was so intense and powerful that I could feel it penetrating my chest area as if his stare was going right through me.

I was transfixed and helpless. I wanted to cry out for my wife to help me, but she was in the next room fast asleep, apparently oblivious to this amazing meeting. Yet I knew that this encounter was not for Denise. No, this was between them and me. I felt vulnerable and defenseless as the three angels scrutinized me.

It was the one in the middle who must have been the leader. I say this because his gaze was so strong that I could just feel him. It was as if he were saying, "That's right Joel, we said we were coming, and here we are. So you know who we are, don't you?" I was helpless. At one point, the angels on the ends moved. They didn't walk, but glided simultaneously, repositioning themselves at the outer edges of my eyesight so that I could hardly see them (one to the left and one to the right), while the "leader" stayed directly in front of me, as if to hold me there frozen. He was still poised with his hand underneath his chin unwavering, staring into me. Momentarily, the two others glided back to their previous positions, each alongside the leader. Then the three began to appear to shrink and fade smaller and smaller, fading until they were no longer in sight. This encounter took maybe one and a half, no more than two minutes. Though no words had been verbalized between us, this incredible phenomenon spoke volumes.

I was now able to move. I was sweating. I began stammering and pacing the floor, wondering to myself what to do. The human mind is a complicated organ. We as humans can be faced with all kinds of visible evidence and still, in our minds we will try to block out the obvious and convince ourselves that we didn't see a thing. Minutes after seeing those angels I remember getting dressed to go to work. I looked over at my wife and decided not to wake her. How could I wake her?

In my mind I began to rationalize, saying, "*Man, you've been married to this woman for so long, you're beginning to think like her.*"

What could I say to her?

"Honey, three angels just visited me, and we had a meeting in the bathroom?" Yeah, right! I decided that I would not tell her or anyone else for that matter, what had transpired. After all, I was a respected sergeant of police. How would it look for a 49-year-old cop to be going around saying he saw three angels?

The more I thought about it, the more I reasoned that I could never mention this to anyone…not even my wife. By the time I arrived at work, I was intent to leave that experience behind me. I had purposed in my mind to move on.

As I put on my uniform and settled in to work, I found myself in a sort of funk. I knew I didn't want to talk about what had happened. But I also knew that it had happened. As much as I wanted to deny seeing those angels, I knew what I saw. I couldn't get away from it. As much as I didn't want to, I found myself sitting in a daze, unable to truly focus on my duties. I was wrestling with this issue in my head, when suddenly my office phone rang.

"Sergeant Jones," I answered.

It was my wife, Denise. She called because she had awakened earlier to discover that I had left without awakening her and giving her a kiss goodbye. She had a right to be upset, because one thing most officers try to do is to make sure we express our love for our family before heading off to work, because in law enforcement you never know if you will ever see your family again.

I remember her saying, "You didn't kiss me goodbye before you left."

I said, "Oh, something came up."

Then for some unknown reason, I asked her,

"Hey have you heard from our *friends* today?"

Denise said, "No, I just woke up." She then said "Why... did something happen?"

Exasperated, I replied, "Uh no, I was just wondering if you could maybe call them or think about them, or whatever you do to get messages from them."

"Don't make fun of me," she shot back, "You know I don't do anything, *they* contact *me...*"

Suddenly, she said, "Wait a minute Joel...I'm getting a message...it's the angels." Denise now sounded anxious. My heart began racing. I held the phone receiver to my ear not saying a word, and listened, first to the silence and then as my wife began speaking in the monotone voice that I have come to now recognize as a telltale sign of her engaging in divine communication.

She began... *"They're saying, tell Joel...we... didn't ...mean.... to spy on him...but ...we had to ...search the deepest...parts...of his heart...because God* has a …plan for you…and …Jesus is coming…to…you.*"*

Denise's normal voice came back and she excitedly screamed in my ear, "Did you see something Joel!?"

By now I couldn't contain it any longer. I didn't want to admit to seeing those three angels. I tried not to, but I finally broke down, crying, sobbing aloud, sniffing and stuttering, admitting to her that indeed, I had a visitation by three angels while she slept.

Denise was overjoyed at this news. Vindicated, she screamed loudly into the phone, "Wooeee…I told you I wasn't crazy! I told you…I told you they were angels….*now* will you believe me?"

I was in my office, slumped over the phone, crying. The intense emotional morning had taken its toll. It was as if I had been wrestling a giant who was twisting my arm and was finally forced to yell, "Uncle!"

In all the excitement, I had forgotten that I was at work and had left my office door open. I looked up with my eyes now red and bloodshot from crying, only to see co-workers quickly moving past my doorway, after possibly eavesdropping. At that moment, it didn't really matter. It was now out. I had admitted to seeing three angels.

"What's next?" I wondered. I would eventually learn that this was but a small introduction to what God had in store for my wife and me.

Call to Me, and I will answer you and show you great and mighty things which you do not know (Jer 33:3).

The next few days, I was pretty messed up. I was so overwhelmed by the fact that I had witnessed these angels with my own two eyes. It was one thing for my wife to have what she sincerely believed to be communications with angelic beings, but it was another thing entirely, for me to *see* these angels. My personal encounter and spiritual awakening, completely messed me up.

This revelation had a huge impact on my life for a variety of reasons. I was never one to really believe in ghosts and the paranormal to any great extent, so it put me in a position to have to rethink a number of things about my life. As far as I was concerned, I was one who needed direct evidence if I was expected to believe in something. Well, the meeting with those three angels served as evidence. You see, if cops don't understand anything else, they understand evidence. No *evidence*...no *case*! For me to see these angels was huge in relation to my belief that angels do in fact exist. This event was a game changer.

This posed a whole different set of possibilities.

"*If angels were real*," I wondered, could it be that this *Jesus* was real?

This was a question that I dared not ask.

You see, I didn't want the answer to be yes.

66

Now you may be wondering why I didn't want the answer to be yes. Well, if Jesus were real, that would mean that my entire life was an out and out lie. I had never believed in Christianity. I would at times make fun of Christians, albeit much of my cynicism was borne out of observing Christians behaving badly (i.e. smoking, drinking, cursing, partying, cheating, having sex, and everything else just as we non-Christians were doing). I didn't go to church and had never read the bible. Neither had I ever required my family to read the bible or to go to a church service.

I also considered preachers to be pompous, slick-talking con men who used a book that was written by some puritan phonies in order to control weak, desperate, and naïve dreamers. I believed that a preacher's only purpose was to fleece congregations and keep people stuffing money in their pockets and believing in some hocus-pocus god. I remember thinking, if Jesus was really God, why would He have to die, and how could He die? It didn't make a bit of sense to me. But, here I was, absolutely reeling after this encounter with angels. I couldn't help but think that they said Jesus was coming to us.

My wife was overjoyed with that prospect, but as for me… I was in no hurry to meet Jesus because I had been living a double life. On the one hand, I was a hard working officer, known for handling dangerous criminals. I was highly skilled and had even attained a reputation among my peers at a tough, metropolitan police department. I was a dutiful husband and father, and had helped to raise two intelligent children. But there was also a dark side to me. I had been extremely unfaithful. When it came to other women who were readily available, another side of me came to the surface. It was as if that same drive that was in me that enabled me to excel in sports and police work also served to fuel me when it came to contact with the opposite sex. Just as there was always a different crime caper to challenge me, there also seemed to always be a female -other than my wife- just as eager for a challenge, an adventure.

I now know that Satan knows our weaknesses. Mine was never liquor, drugs, or even gambling, but deception and adultery through gratifying my flesh. So after facing the possibility that Jesus really did exist, I began agonizing about Jesus coming to me.

"Why me?" I thought.

"He couldn't possibly want to speak to me. I'm the last person to ever want to be a Christian. This doesn't make any sense at all. This will only cause trouble. What if my wife finds out about my lack of self-control? I have guns all over the house," I thought. *"She'd kill me. What if my children found out? Heck, they might kill me!"*

I was besieged with these thoughts day in and day out. It's funny that although I was hardly a Christian, and I knew virtually nothing about Jesus, I reckoned in my mind that if He were real…then I would have to really honor Him. I reasoned that I would not be able to walk with and speak with Jesus unless I was willing to be changed.

In retrospect, I now understand that Jesus sought me out because He knew that I would be obedient to the changes He would require of me. I would soon learn that Jesus would not only make requirements of me, but my wife as well.

"Then the Commander of the LORD's army said to Joshua, 'Take your sandal off your foot, for the place where you stand is holy.' And Joshua did so." (Joshua 5:15)

CHAPTER SEVEN

You Only Feel Pain When You Return

It had been about 4-5 days since my encounter with the angels. I had come to the conclusion that I had no solution to the problem that I was facing. It was no doubt a supernatural predicament. I found myself reasoning that if Jesus did truly exist, and truly had a plan for me – as the angels said – then surely He would help me to keep my secret sins hidden from my wife. Man, did I have it all wrong.

Have you ever been so worried about something that you just worry yourself to sleep? That's what happened to me. I was like a human ostrich, just trying to bury my head in the ground in hopes that when I awoke this predicament would be over.

It was late one evening, and as I agonized over what was going on in my life with these angels, I was lying on the sofa in my living room. I was watching TV, but my mind was so preoccupied that I had fallen asleep, only to be awakened about an hour later. I felt someone nudging my shoulder saying,

"Joel, wake up!" Denise said.

She appeared fearful and was crying softly.

She then said, "The angels are here...they're telling me that I have to repent of my sins. Joel they're telling me everything I've done in my life, and guess what? They're telling me things about *you* Joel, things about you and women!"

I was shocked! At first, I just stared dumbfounded.

I thought, *"Oh no!"* My worst fears have come to pass.

Although I knew I had been unfaithful at times, I could only shake my head, and stammer, "No," in repudiation of the truth.

Denise continued crying, saying, "Joel, they're saying you've done things with women. I told them you wouldn't hurt me like that...that you wouldn't do anything like that."

I denied it, saying, "I didn't do anything."

I desperately disavowed my infidelity. I knew that if I admitted my wrongdoing, the trust she had in me was likely to evaporate before my eyes along with any real meaning in our 30-year marriage.

It would never be the same. *"Thirty years of marriage, out the window... gone,"* I thought. Hurriedly, I sat up from the couch, repeating that it wasn't true, signifying that these angels were liars.

Her face streaming tears, Denise said, "They say we have to come to the bedroom because Jesus is here."

I was absolutely petrified at what she said. I slowly stood up from the couch, and grabbed Denise's hand.

We both turned toward the bedroom and began what seemed like a mile long death walk. As we headed for the bedroom, Denise continued sobbing. She was still in shock over the accusations of my infidelity. I was angry with the angels, yet I was so afraid.

I thought to myself, *"Why would they do this? Why would they hurt Denise like this and ruin my marriage?"* But in fact the unfortunate situation was my fault.

Even Denise wondered…later admitting to me that she was saying to herself, "These can't be 'good' angels, because they're lying about my husband."

I found myself agonizing on the words that Denise had said, "They say *Jesus* is here."

I had been in violent police situations in my life, yet had never really lost my composure. But in that moment, as Denise and I approached the bedroom of our house, I found myself nearly unable to breathe due to anticipation and anxiety.

74

What would I find in our bedroom? I had seen three angelic beings a few days ago; I could only imagine what might be awaiting us this time. Denise and I clung to each other, both now whimpering and crying like two disobedient children fearing discipline from their parents.

I didn't know it then, but I now know that in His word, Jesus says,

"Assuredly I say to you, unless you are converted and become as little children you will by no means enter the kingdom of heaven." (Matt 18:3)

So we walked for what seemed like an eternity, the 20-35 steps into our bedroom. Arriving in the bedroom, Denise paused again, looking at me through tear filled eyes.

"Joel, they said you've done things with other women."

I could only put my index finger to my mouth and utter, "Shsssh," in an effort to quiet her. For while my ears were hearing her, my eyes were darting left to right, surveying the room for a quick security inventory. After all, I reasoned, if I ever had any previous unbelief about the supernatural, I now knew beyond a doubt that there were angels among us. But nothing could prepare me for what was about to occur.

As I cautiously scanned the room, my eyes settled on Denise and I noticed a drastic difference in her. I witnessed Denise's face and body change. She raised her head and looked me straight in the eyes. Her posture was no longer slumping as if defeated. Her shoulders were no longer rounded and heavy. Her tears had stopped, and she stood up straight, facing me, nearly at attention. Denise had taken on the appearance of a soldier about to report. Focusing her stare on me with keen defiance in her eyes, she opened her mouth, and what came out was a powerful...*voice.*

It was not her voice, but a male voice. It was a voice nearly as deep as mine. It was a strong, baritone voice.

In a distinct and assertive tone, the voice asked, "Now Joel Jones, did you do 'such and such' with 'so and so' or didn't you?" Before I could even respond, the voice continued, "You wouldn't do anything like that, would you? Or, would you? Why don't you tell *us*, Joel Jones?"

I was dumbfounded! Okay…what was happening here? Number 1, how could my wife be speaking in such a manly voice? Number 2, how could she know about the last affair that I had? Number 3, who was this *"us"* to whom the voice was referring? Denise stood there, eyeballing me intently. I thought to myself, "Don't buy into this. She's trying to fool you into admitting that you cheated on her. It's a trick!!"

I found myself looking around her, and then examining the area behind her. I was desperately searching for a recording device, or, maybe one of those new fangled voice-box gizmos that singers use to change the sound of their voice. Still, she just stared directly at me, undaunted, as if to say, *your move.*

Her eyes were clear and confident. I searched my mind...but logic couldn't help me...common reason had abandoned me...I could not find one viable explanation for what I was witnessing. And so, I did what I had learned through a life encompassing 20 years of police work and 49 years of living without God in my life... I lied.

I sheepishly said, "I haven't done anything."

I often think about what transpired after I told that lie. I sincerely believe to this day that God used that lie as a way of formally introducing me to Jesus. For it was after I responded with a lie that I then heard His voice distinctly say to me, "Son, do you know who I am? I'm God! I'm the same God of Abraham, Isaac and Jacob. I knew the hairs on your head before I formed the earth. Now what I have is a plan for you and Denise, and it starts right here, right now, today, but you must repent your sins."

God then said to me, "Denise has been put away. I have put her in a place and I am occupying this space." He continued, "You see, son, I am a Spirit. As Spirit, I can move into two people, or two million people, or a number you don't even know." He told me that He could do that because He was God. He then told me something so incredible that it solidified my faith; removing any immediate doubt that I may have had during our conversation.

"Why do you think I brought you back when you drowned?" The Lord then paused, as if giving me a chance to digest what He had just said.

Wait a minute… something was happening. As I looked at Denise, the Lord was using her body, her head slowly nodding at me. At that moment my mind raced back to my youth, to the age of fourteen, and just like that, I was back in school. That was the year I had a harrowing experience in my high school swimming pool. I had just entered high school and was attending my first swim class.

As we boys were undressing in the locker room, a few of the guys in my class asked out loud who could swim and who couldn't. I don't recall how many could actually swim, but when they asked me, I told them that I could swim. Of course I couldn't, but peer pressure being what it was, I succumbed to misplaced pride. Yes, folks, pride is an ingredient Satan uses from birth, which is at the root of all sin. On this occasion, pride of course caused me to lie. So, once I said I could swim, they dared me to jump in. So that one lie precipitated my next move.

What else could I do? I was committed at that point I (as they say, I had to "own it"). So I did. I closed my eyes, and leapt into the pool. I figured I had seen tons of *Tarzan* movies, and it seemed so easy when that actor who used to play Tarzan (the late Johnny Weismuller), would yell "Agghhheeeaah" and swim across the water saving whoever was in distress. If he could swim, so could I. Well, I quickly discovered that I wasn't Tarzan, and swimming in water was a lot more difficult than walking on dry land (Duh, ya think?).

I wound up in the deep end of the high school swimming pool. I went under, tumbling upside down and fighting frantically in the deep water, rising briefly...only long enough to cry out for help (where was *Tarzan* now, because I was certainly in distress). Once I was in the pool, the others in the pool paid little attention to me. It was a large pool and many were splashing, yelling and frolicking in the water. But I was seriously drowning. I quickly lost my breath and sank deep into the depths of the pool. I remembered thinking "*I'm going to drown.*" I had always considered drowning to be the worst way a person could die, and wouldn't you know it...it was happening to me. I was deep under the water upside down. My thrashing and struggling while exhaling caused me to lose my breath even quicker. I remember thinking, "*What happens when I run out of air...how does it feels to actually die?*" Well, I soon found out.

As I drank that pool's water, I lost my last breath, and.... I felt instant peace. It was as if I was traveling underwater. I could still think and reason. I wondered what was happening.

I thought, "*I know I've drowned, so why am I still able to think? And where is my body?*" I was fervently examining myself, looking for what I could remember being embodied with...arms, legs, and so forth. I couldn't see my body. I remember going toward a light, but as I neared that light my traveling began to slow down, similar to a subway train coming to a stop. It was then that I began hearing voices in the distance yelling,

"Pull him out! Roll him over, press his stomach." The voices became clearer, their instructions louder... and Bam!! Coughing and throwing up water, I regained consciousness.

I discovered I was out of the water, lying on the side of the pool, staring up at 4-5 people who it turns out had fished me out of the water.

They were saying, "Are you okay? You almost drowned."

So all my life from the age of 14 to 49, I had gone through life thinking I had almost died.

But now…back in the present… in my bedroom in the fall of 2004, the Lord asked, "Why do you think I brought you back when you drowned?"

I began to speak, saying, "But I didn't…" Immediately my words were cut off. God stared at me through my wife's skin, and the Lord said to me, "Oh, but you *did* die, Joel."

"Your soul was coming to me, but it wasn't your time. If I had taken you then, you would never have been able to fulfill the purpose that I have for you. You would never have met Denise. You see, son, when people first die, they don't even know they're dead, because you don't feel any pain when you die. You only feel pain if you return."

For a moment God was silent. He of course knew my finite mind. He gave me a few seconds to digest what had just occurred, reliving those moments when I had died, sensing the events all over again. But instead of being that frightened 14-year-old boy back in 1969, God was allowing me to examine my past in the present year

83

of 2004 in His holy presence, in order to prove to me that He was indeed God.

I looked at my wife's face and her head slowly began to nod. Her mouth showed a hint of a smile as if the Lord were saying, "Now that you really know who I am, let's move on."

Of course I now had no doubt that He was God. The Lord then resumed His questioning of me "Now Joel Jones, did you do this?" Quietly...very quietly, in tears I answered, "Yes."

I knew He was referring to my unfaithfulness.

He then said, "Son, I am God, you must bow to me and say, "Yes, Lord.'"

I did as instructed. I bowed my head and said, "Yes, Lord." The Lord began questioning me about my various episodes of unfaithfulness, each time asking me in a clear voice, "Did you do this, Joel Jones?" Each time I bowed and answered affirmatively, "Yes, Lord." After

84

what seemed like an eternity, but in reality must have been about 30-45 minutes, the Lord said, "Most of your sins are the same. They are sins of the flesh."

He then said something that I often think about.

"But don't worry, son. I am going to forgive you, and I'm going to bless you and Denise and your children's, children's, children and all the people you love."

At that point, I had no way of knowing that the word of God says in 1 John 1:9,

"If we confess our sins, He is faithful and just to forgive us our sins and cleanse us of all unrighteousness."

It was uncanny, but as I stood in His presence, I could actually feel my past and sordid desires leaving my body.

They seemed to travel vertically upward, along the inside of my body and out through the top of my head.

85

A lifetime of cravings and desires were drawn upwards from the pit of my loins out through the top of my head. God had begun cleansing me of unrighteousness, just as His word describes in the Holy bible. God was cleaning house. Hallelujah!

The Lord continued speaking out of my wife. He began to give me specific instructions.

"You and Denise will no longer sing R&B, but you will write and sing gospel/inspirational music. I will send you the music. You will travel the country and the world spreading My word through testimony and song."

He also said that many would be saved because of our testimony. He continued speaking to me...this time saying, a relative of ours will become an attorney and work for His kingdom. The Lord then said, "Read my word from cover to cover. Anything you don't understand, I will reveal it to you. Pray daily and go to church."

He instructed us to attend a nearby church. He gave us the name of the church, and said of the pastor there, "He is a humble servant of mine."

I was absolutely overwhelmed. I had so many questions to ask, but I didn't know where to begin. It was all so astonishing and coming at me so fast. First of all, how and why would I write gospel music? I had never sung a gospel song in my life, nor did I know any, not even *Amazing Grace.* Denise and I were R&B singers. We were known on stage as *Dee & Jay.* We would travel around the Bay Area and beyond, providing music and a party atmosphere wherever needed. We did clubs and hotel venues.

Dee was sometimes called the instant party package (just book us at your event and a party was bound to develop). I had seen the staunchest, most reserved crowds of people turn into the loosest party animals, wildly dancing atop tables once my wife and I began singing and performing. We were in popular demand for birthdays, anniversaries, and corporate functions, as well as Christmas parties…you name it.

87

We were the rave on cruise ships, and we were also in popular demand at Halloween and at New Year's Eve parties. We were reveling in the throes of the secular music scene, and the decadence that comes with it. Needless to say, neither of us had any plans to sing gospel music, let alone to write gospel music. But as is mentioned in Gen 50:20, what was meant for evil (by the devil) God would use for good.

Again, I had so many questions in my mind that I wanted to ask God, but I thought it better that I just listen so that I could get it all down and follow His instructions. I really wanted to ask God about the part where He named a specific relative of ours, saying that this person would become an attorney. This of course would cost both money and preparation, and neither Denise's family nor mine had any real money to speak of. Our relative attended a public school, where resources were a far cry from the material available to students who attended private schools that prepped them for careers in law.

Yet here was God, very matter-of-factly telling me that these things would in fact take place. Needless to say, my wife and I would live to see that (like clockwork), within the next few years that is exactly what happened. God raised up a lawyer. But how could this be?

Well, in Phil 4:19 scripture tells us that "*My God shall supply all your needs according to His riches in glory by Christ Jesus.*" God continued to astound us. Upon graduating from law school, amazingly, our relative passed one of the toughest State Bar Exams in the country on the very first try.

You see, when God has a plan for your life, *He sets the wheels in motion long before you arrive.* I have learned that when God makes promises He intends to keep them. He is extravagant and does things in a big way. Romans 4:17 reminds us *that it is God who gives life to the dead, and calls those things that do not exist as though they did.* In the case of my kinsman's career, God had not only called it, before it came to be, but also referenced it as if it had already existed.

89

To this day, I am convinced that this law career was preordained by the hand of God. I am certainly not worthy, but am so honored that He chose to give me that revelation. Amazing!

CHAPTER EIGHT

A SPIN AROUND THE BLOCK

Back in that bedroom in the fall of 2004 the Lord said to me, "Joel, we now have a covenant. I will not break this covenant, only you can." I was so far from knowing God or the bible at the time that I remember not even understanding what He meant by having a covenant with Him. Later, through the guidance and teaching received from the Holy Spirit, I would learn that this was the same type of relationship that God had extended to Abraham and his descendants: a binding agreement, an eternal covenant relationship. What an honor! What a privilege!

The Lord continued to give us instructions that night, using my wife as a vessel. It was so surreal that even as I am writing this book nearly 8 years later, I am still completely awestruck at the wonder of God. How the Creator of the world can love His creation so much that He is willing to even inhabit the body of one's spouse in order to get the other's attention. To me that is incredible. But to God... it's all in a day's work (or maybe even a second's work). After all, didn't He speak to His prophet Moses through a burning bush (Exodus 3)? The Lord even caused a donkey to speak to Balaam, a sorcerer who practiced divination (Numbers 22). I am convinced that we serve a God in Jesus Christ who longs to speak to and commune with His children daily. He has a plethora of ways to get our attention. As you read further, you will see that God speaks to us all daily, using different methods of communication, and different vessels depending on the importance of the message He needs to convey. God conveys truth to the listener.

Therefore, it is vitally important for one's ears to be open to the voice of the Lord. 2 Chr 16:9 says,

"The eyes of the Lord search to and fro, across the entire earth, seeking to show Himself strong on behalf of those whose hearts are truly turned to Him."

AnnaLisa and I have learned that strict obedience, even to the smallest details, is of the utmost importance if one is to have an intimate relationship with the Lord, and realize all that He has for them.

As the bible mentions in 1 Sam 15: 22,

"To obey is better than sacrifice, and to heed than the fat of rams."

And so, the Lord continued speaking. As one might expect, I was nervous and unsure, yet at one point I sheepishly asked, "Why me, Lord?" He answered, "Out of your generation, I knew that you would be obedient." He then said, "Now get some rest, for we have a lot of work to do." I had no idea what He meant by that. I surmised that He meant out of the generation of my family. I had no idea what was to come. But what I did know was that from that moment on, our lives could never be the same.

"I beseech you brethren, by the mercies of God that you present your bodies as a living sacrifice, holy and acceptable to God, which is our reasonable service. And do not be conformed to this world, but be

93

transformed by the renewing of your mind, that you may prove what is that good, and acceptable, and perfect will of God." (Romans 12:1-2)

After the Lord had told me to rest (because there was much work ahead), Denise's posture immediately returned to normal. The erect military style body language gave way to a softer, less secure stance. I searched her eyes and could see that the keen intense stare which I had observed in her eyes during the time the Lord had taken her over was now replaced with my wife's familiar and more curious, wide eyed look. I noticed her eyes darting up and down and around as if taking inventory of herself. I found myself peering into her eyes, asking "Denise....is that you?" Denise acknowledged me and seemed to nod slightly. However, she was obviously very unsettled and afraid. Any normal human being would be terrified, considering that the Lord of creation had decided to enter her body, use it as a vessel, and take it for a spin around the block. I had to ask her, "Honey, did you hear anything that just happened?"

Oh …why did I ask that? Indeed she had heard every word. You see, my confession to the Lord was received through His vessel, which was Denise. God had used her as a human antenna or conduit in order to converse with me. Therefore, Denise had clearly heard of all my adulterous escapades. She now knew that I had lived a double life.

Thirty years of trust in someone who was considered a husband and friend had proved to be 30 years of deception. Denise's emotions ricocheted, bouncing to and fro, from hurt and fear to unbridled anger and disgust. She had just come out of a darkened hell in the spiritual realm only to confront a new hell in the natural, face to face with someone that she had trusted for 30 years of her life. Jesus had shown her who I had been for 30 years, an ungodly demon possessed sinner. Denise had trusted me implicitly.

But the word of God says, *"Cursed is the man who trusts in man and makes flesh his strength, whose heart departs from the Lord."* (Jeremiah 17:5)

Denise had returned to a husband who was now a stranger to her. What would become of our marriage? How could she ever trust me again? As I look back, I know that God could have worked things out so that my confessing my sins were done out of earshot of my wife. But that's not God's way. Luke 12:1-3 speaks to the fact that what is in darkness will be brought to light.

I really wasn't ready for the answer she gave me. In answer to my question about if she had heard anything as the Lord and I spoke to one another, Denise said, "I could hear you and another person talking, but I couldn't speak. I was in a dark place." She began to weep softly, saying, "Joel, I didn't like that feeling, I don't want to go back there." I held onto her. We clung to each other. I felt helpless. I wouldn't have wanted to be in Denise's position either, but I would have taken her place had God allowed me. I could only imagine what a harrowing situation that must have been for her. Since the age of 14, she had considered me her protector, yet here I was, when she needed me most, and all I could do was to stand by, helpless and afraid.

My wife had just gone through something so unbelievably mind blowing, yet I was powerless to do anything about it. I felt useless. We were like two lost children needing to find our way back home. I know that it was God's plan to do just that, to reclaim us as His children, children of God. The God of Abraham, Isaac and Jacob…the great I AM, the Lord had sent the Son of God, Jesus Christ the Lord to deliver us both.

Denise would be used as a chosen vessel of God's (a 'burning bush' of sorts) through which He would get my attention and our repentance. With repentance and transformation come purging, and both Denise and I would discover in the next few days and years that the purging process was only just beginning.

"I know a man in Christ who fourteen years ago-whether in the body I do not know, or whether out of the body I do not know, God knows-such a one was caught up to the third heaven." (2 Corinthians 12:2)

The next six days of our lives were truly indescribable. I can only say that God Himself is the only one who can give you total explanation and reason for what Denise and I saw and experienced in those six days. Of course, it is with supplication and prayer to our Lord and Savior Jesus Christ that we enlist His aid in everything we say and do. So with the power of His Holy Spirit I will recount to you -the reader- what transpired.

That same night that the Lord had told us to get some rest, we were visited by Him again. It was approximately 2:30AM. Denise and I had both fallen asleep, still uneasy, considering the day's events. I was awakened by Denise who was lying on her side beside me nudging me.

I heard a voice say "Joel, wake up." It was a familiar voice, *but not Denise's voice.* I woke with a start, immediately recognizing the voice as the voice of God. As He had previously done, the Lord had manifested Himself in Denise. I could only stare at Denise as His voice spoke to me. The Lord began talking as if we were old friends. He began telling me about heaven and hell. He told me that Denise was now in a dark place where

98

there was biting and suffering, and gnashing of teeth. He told me that she was His daughter and that He loved her very much. He said He had to send her to this place for a reason.

He then said, "If I send her here Joel, just imagine where I will send you." Amazingly, I could hear moaning and crying, coming from this place of darkness. At one point I could hear the voice of a very close acquaintance, who had been like family to Denise and I.

This person happened to have been murdered in a shooting at least five years prior to Jesus coming to us, and did not know the Lord at the time of his death. This person was in the same place as Denise and wondered what Denise was doing there. The Lord told me that Denise was being guided through this place. I pray that as you readers read this excerpt that the Lord makes it clear to you.

As the Lord was speaking to me, I could hear Denise's voice pleading to Him, "Father, they're biting me, they're biting me." The Lord would then calm her, instructing her which way to go; He said very reassuringly, "Daughter, walk this way, you're almost out."

He then told me that she was nearing the opening of this place. Although I was still in bed staring at Denise's body, I could visualize her walking in the darkness, terrified. I myself seemed to be waiting outside of this place, which was outer darkness. After several minutes of talking to me and guiding Denise's footsteps left and right, the Lord said to me,

"Okay Joel, she's almost out. Now grab her hand and pull downward toward the foot of the bed and she will be out."

What is uncanny is that while we were in the spirit, the Lord could easily move us in and out from the spirit back to the natural, in our bedroom. He continued instructing me, patiently imploring me to pull Denise's hand in order to assist in freeing her from this place in the spirit realm back to the natural realm. His speech was similar to a doctor directing a mother during the birthing process,

"Alright son, she's... almost out...walk this way Denise...pull steady Joel, downward now... toward the foot of the bed."

The Lord then said that she was nearly out. He said that He would see us again the following night.

He said, "Denise will be cold when she comes out, so wrap her in the covers when she is out. I will see you again tomorrow."

With that, I witnessed Denise's body shivering, almost to the point of convulsing. She was back in her natural body. Her teeth were chattering. I quickly wrapped the bed's covers around her and held her tight, asking her if she was okay.

She could barely speak. Her teeth were chattering and she said, "They were biting me, they were biting me...I couldn't see them, and they just kept biting me." Denise said that the smell of that place was so dreadful

101

that she could still smell the stench even days after being there. Both my wife and I have come to have some of our most intimate and enlightening meetings with God during these times in the wee hours of the morning.

I am not ashamed to say that although I had very little fear of anything before I met the Lord; I now fear nothing except the Lord. It is not the type of fear that comes over you like when you face a sinister or evil person, or even a life-threatening situation. Rather, it is a reverent fear that reminds you that you are in the holy presence of the Creator of the entire universe. The same God who not only measured the waters of the sea in the hollow of His hand (Is 40:12), but who holds the very life of every living thing and the breath of all mankind in His hand. (Job 12:10)

God is accessible and easy to talk to, yet because of my reverent fear of and respect for God, after noticing that He never volunteered any further information as to why He sent Denise to this awful place, I suppose it took me years to ask Him about His reasons for doing so.

102

It may benefit readers to know that just recently my wife and I both prayed and then asked the Lord just what was that place, and why was Denise sent there? The Lord spoke to us both. This time He spoke to us via divine writing, addressing Himself by using the pronoun "We" (in reference to the triune Godhead).

The writing came back as follows;

"We have dungeons full of angels who have misbehaved, and have been cast into dungeons of darkness. We say yes, yes, yes, yes, yes, yes. Our daughter (Denise) had to visit this outer darkness. Why? Because it exists. We took her there. We said while she is there she will feel a coldness, a void, a place absent from the presence of God. It is a place that has no love, a place that has all the meanings of hell. We had her visit this outer darkness so that she can tell the world that God's justice is *God's* justice. If one disobeys and dies in one's sins, here they will be cast for all eternity. The 'fire' Denise did not witness, because God gave *that* testimony to someone other than her."

103

"Behold, I stand at the door and knock. If anyone hears My voice and opens the door, I will come in to him and dine with him, and he with Me." (Revelation 3:20)

During the next six days the Lord daily visited Denise and me. At times we would be together at home seated on the couch conversing, trying to make sense of all the supernatural things that were occurring in our lives -and just like that- the Lord would visit us. Of course we were still in shock over what had happened a day ago at the meeting with Jesus.

We would be visited by the great I AM. As I said before, one way the I AM would speak to me was by manifesting Himself in Denise's body.

No warning, no introduction, He would simply take her over. Now I've often heard other Christ followers say that God has a sense of humor. Well...I can certainly tell you that He does. There was an occasion during the week after Jesus had spoken to me in the bedroom when Denise and I decided to go out to breakfast. We were still reeling over all that was going on, and just needed to have a meal in public, in proximity to other people.

I guess we just wanted to feel that nothing had really changed in our lives. We arrived at this restaurant and were seated and quietly eating. I remember that we were not conversing at the time. I was deep in thought, still pondering what was transpiring in our lives. I imagine Denise was doing the same. I remember looking down at my omelet and cutting into it with my fork when all of a sudden, the silence was broken.

I heard that distinct voice say, "Look what they've done to My food. You see Joel, that's another reason I have to come back. This food is terrible; it is not supposed to be this way."

I raised my head in shock. I had sat down with my wife to eat, only to look up and witness her seated across from me looking like anything but a woman. Don't get me wrong, I was in the company of Denise's flesh, but again God was using her as a vessel. Whenever the

Lord would manifest Himself in her, her mannerisms would change to that of a masculine male.

He continued talking about how sin had entered the world. He gave me a brief history of a fallen world, in desperate need of Jesus' return. Please understand that this was during the first couple of weeks after our encounter with Jesus. We would later learn that God can and will speak to you in a variety of ways. But during this time He chose to use Denise as a vessel – as I said – to get my undivided attention, and wow, did it work!

I don't remember ever finishing my breakfast that morning in the restaurant. I was too in awe at what was going on. Transfixed, I just stared and listened. I remember the Lord speaking to me as we stood up to leave the table. He extended His hand (Denise's hand), and I did in kind. He grabbed my hand and we shook hands.

He looked me in the eye, and said to me "Joel, you have a good firm handshake. Now be sure to tip the waitress." He then strode toward the door in a walk more akin to John Wayne than Denise. I stood open mouthed, frantically fumbling through my pocket in an effort to retrieve the proper amount of money for a tip. I then hurried toward the door of the restaurant in an attempt to rejoin my wife.

As I mentioned earlier, the Lord would also speak to us through divine writings, which were messages that the Lord would send to us through Denise's hand and finger. As Denise and I began delving deeper into the bible, being led by the Holy Spirit, God continued to be true to His word. As I said previously, He had told us to read His word from cover to cover. He added that anything we didn't understand, He would reveal to us.

I remember reading in the New Testament, John 8:5-7, about Jesus being confronted by the scribes and Pharisees. They sought to test Him concerning a woman who had committed the sin of adultery, asking, "What do You say?"

The Bible says that Jesus then stooped down and wrote on the ground with His finger, as if He did not hear.

He then raised Himself up and said to them, "He who is without sin among you, let him throw a stone at her first."

In the Old Testament book of Daniel, chapter 5:5, it tells of a man's hand actually appearing and writing on the wall in the king's presence. This was amazing. I have since spoken to some Christ followers who said they also write. They call it journaling.

Now I certainly am not questioning if my fellow believers are receiving correspondence from the Lord, but I can only say to anyone out there who feels that he or she is being led by the Lord, to *test the spirit* as the Bible instructs in 1 John 4:1. You must do this in order to know who is speaking to you. The great I AM, the God of Abraham, Isaac and Jacob, the Ancient of days was speaking to us. Early on, He even taught us how to discern with whom we were speaking. He said,

"Whenever you want to receive written, divine messages from me, you must first rebuke all evil spirits, because Satan and his demons can come through as well."

The Lord said that when they are rebuked in Jesus' name demons have to flee. He took us up in the spirit and would allow unclean spirits to come our way and approach us. The Lord would drill me, telling me to rebuke the unclean spirits. They would have to flee. The Lord told us that demons have to flee at the name of Jesus Christ. During this time of being caught up in the spirit, I could hear these demons and evil spirits asking that I not rebuke them. The Lord also said that if we wanted correspondence from Him we were to first open our bibles and locate scripture from His word. He would then speak to us through excerpts in His word. We then were to rebuke all demonic spirits in the name of Jesus and we would pray. This was to be done by my wife and me prior to receiving any divine writings from Him.

Once we followed the proper protocol outlined by the Lord, only then would He speak to us via divine writing. The Lord said that this was one of the gifts that

109

He had given Denise. He said she had received this gift because her heart was pure and this gift will be for us to use as long as she is on the earth.

I should explain that later in our walk with God, He explained that although Denise's heart was termed pure, she was by no means perfect. No human being has "arrived" or attained perfection; and as long as we are in this earthly body the need to be shaped and transformed into the image of God will be a continuous one.

The Lord further explained that He knows the hearts of His children. We think we know what's in our hearts, but only God actually knows. He said He knew our hearts before He formed us, and although none of us are perfect and all of us need work, Denise was one of His vessels whose heart certainly belonged to Him. The Lord said that this gift is a very precious and powerful gift because it affords us access to the Creator at any time, assuring us that He will answer. Having access to the Lord in this manner removes any guesswork as to if He is speaking to us. We simply have to obey His commands.

He told us that not many people could be entrusted with this gift. The Lord said this gift is so special that many might be tempted -due to the flesh of man- to misuse it. God guaranteed Denise and I that He will not take this gift away until Denise comes to her true home, which is heaven. I should say that I had never read the bible at the time we were receiving much of this information, so you can imagine my astonishment concerning some of the things that I was hearing. After all, I was an officer and I was taught that in order to prove a case there needed to be evidence. Circumstantial evidence at least, direct evidence at best. God already knew what I was thinking. He had a plan and provided proof for my every thought.

This was an amazing amount of information and supernatural events that He was throwing at Denise and me. But to Him it was just a drop in the bucket.

Now, ever since the Lord decided to come into our lives He has communed with Denise and me daily. The Holy Spirit has been leading and guiding us for the last 8 years. We now know and better understand how

God works in the lives of His people, those willing to be pruned, transformed, consecrated, and set apart.

The word of God says in 2 Peter 1:20-21,

"No prophesy of scripture is of any private interpretation. For prophecy never came by the will of man, but holy men of god spoke as they were carried by the Holy Spirit."

The Lord was honing and transforming my wife and me into vessels of honor: sanctified and useful for the Master, prepared for every good work (2 Timothy 2:21). Clearly, God is immutable and unchanging. His plan for mankind is going forth and cannot be derailed by the forces of darkness. God's bible is complete. There is nothing that will be added or taken away lest those who do so be accursed and condemned (Galatians 1:8-9; Revelation 22:18-19).

CHAPTER NINE

Two Weeks

"Then we who are alive, who are left, will be caught up together with them in the clouds to meet the Lord in the air, and so we will always be with the Lord." (1 Thessalonians 4:17)

The next few days would prove to be even *more* amazing. The Lord continued to move us even more in the spirit. It was on one of these occasions that the Lord gave us a very strong vision. Denise received a vision of the rapture. There were people who had just arrived in what could only have been heaven. These people were scrambling around, excitedly searching for others who they had known.

It was as if they were in an intake area of heaven, transitioning in life from one dimension to another. Many were Denise's family members, meeting up in this place in the sky. Those who were in the vision being "raptured up" seemed as astonished as Denise and I was as we viewed this vision; and listened with rapt attention.

Family members were asking, "Have you seen so and so?" This vision also showed fire and great rocks falling away from the earth. Buildings were being destroyed. There was great turmoil and destruction on the earth, while those who were in heaven were excitedly taking inventory of who had made it up from their former lives. In this vision Jesus was also visiting others who were still on earth. We are not sure about the sequence of this powerful vision. My wife and I have since asked the Lord to clarify certain things that occurred in this magnificent vision, and He has said that it is very important that people know that Jesus gives us all every opportunity to follow Him. Those who choose to do otherwise will suffer greatly.

It was as if the Lord was showing us glimpses of what was to come, but in random order, reminiscent of a collage of future events framed together and come to life. While we were receiving this vision, we were still awake in bed. I was lying next to Denise, and the Lord was speaking to us both through her. As with the time when the Lord had taken Denise into outer darkness and I

114

seemed to be outside listening as God narrated what was occurring, I myself couldn't directly see the people going up, but I could certainly hear them. I could also hear Jesus telling us what was going on in the vision. At certain times I began seeing glimpses as Jesus narrated.

At one point there was a young man who we knew from our old high school. I'll call his name "Van" when referring to him here. Van had passed away quite young, only a few years after graduating. This was back in Chicago around 1975. Van had been a talented and scrappy softball player in my old neighborhood on one of the softball teams called the *Hornets.* Van was also a very popular dancer. People in the area would always comment on his dancing ability.

Well in this vision, Van was dancing in heaven, and the Lord said to me, "You see that young man? He dances all over heaven." How could this be, that although I couldn't actually see Van, I could see him dancing as the Lord narrated to me!? It was as if I was standing outside of this huge room hearing all that was taking place, and seeing brief sightings of these people as the

Lord God spoke it to me. In the same vision, there were people lined up for what seemed like miles and they were all standing there in line, clamoring expectedly.

It reminded me of a scene where people are waiting to enter an event or a store opening and they're all lined up, except that the line seemed to extend for miles.

One man excitedly gestured to me from his place in line, saying, "Joel, we were praying for you; we didn't think you were going to make it." Just then the Lord said to us, "They're lined up for miles, they've all been waiting to see you for a long time. Go and shake their hands."

I remember Denise and I being overjoyed at seeing all of these people; some were friends and relatives. Some were famous celebrities when they were alive on earth. Just think of the many people who have gone on to greater things; many were there, each with their signature voices. I immediately recognized the voices of celebrities because they were big stars while on earth, and some on TV and movies, etc. Yet, even they were reaching to shake our hands as if we were long lost friends and family members. I would later read the bible and discover indeed, that we are all family in heaven. In Luke 15:7,

Jesus says, *"I say to you that likewise there will be more joy in heaven over one sinner who repents than over ninety-nine just persons who need no repentance."*

Indeed, heaven was rejoicing.

"For I know the plans I have for you, declares the Lord, plans to prosper you and not to harm you, plans to give you hope and a future." (Jeremiah 29:11)

In the coming days, the Lord began showing us still more and more amazing things. One day Denise received a very clear vision from the Lord. In the vision, she saw our neighbor exit the house and lie down on the front lawn and pass away. Denise was unnerved by this vision. I asked her why God would choose to send her a

117

vision of that type. What did it mean? Neither of us had an answer. We wouldn't have to ponder for long.

The very next day, upon returning home from work I discovered my neighbors milling around the front of their house. I noticed an ambulance had just left the area. I rushed into our house and saw Denise standing there on the verge of tears. She said, "Joel, the ambulance just left. The lady next door did just what the vision showed. She came outside and lay down on her front lawn. Then the paramedics came and took her away. I think she's dead." Denise was very sad. I noticed the woman's husband sitting dejectedly outside of his house with his head down.

They were fairly new in our neighborhood, and we didn't know them well. Prior to this we hadn't spoken much to them and vice versa. But God is about bringing people together. Denise said we should go over and ask if we could be of help.

I went over to the man and said, "Hello, my wife told me the paramedics came and took your wife away. Is it anything serious? We'd like to offer to pray for her, if that's alright with you."

He said, "That's the best news I've heard all day, but I'm afraid you're too late. She died." I was shocked. Although I didn't know about the gifts of the Holy Spirit at that time, I have since learned that God was proving Himself to us again by extending the gifts of the Holy Spirit's revelations.

This vision Denise had received showing a future event is known as the gift of the *Word of Wisdom*. It is one of the divine gifts of the Holy Spirit whereupon God gives one a word or revelation of future events that only He could know. Great prophets of both the old and new testaments of the bible functioned in this gift. Obviously, God is still willing to show His children future events, especially when His ultimate aim is to save the lost.

It was an amazing supernatural revelation that humbled both my wife and me. To think that God would

119

bless us to receive such a gift is life altering. I couldn't understand why in the vision it showed our neighbor exit the house, close the front door, and then lie down on the front lawn and die. All of a sudden her husband started speaking, explaining to me that he had been at work when his wife phoned him, telling him that she was feeling as if she were going to faint. He told her to call 911. She did so, and decided to wait for the ambulance outside. Her husband said they had cats in their home and the cats frightened easily. His wife thought that if she allowed the paramedics to enter the house, the cats might become alarmed and run outside.

Therefore, after calling 911, she decided to go outside and await the ambulance. Apparently, while sitting out front she had a massive brain aneurism, lapsed into a coma and died. Well, Denise and I ministered to this man, and eventually he and others began attending church.

This vision was just one of several that we would later receive. During this same time period, I received a strong vision that the Lord sent me. I was wide awake reading my bible, when I saw, over my head yet behind me, outside of my window, what appeared to be hundreds of demons marching in formation. These demons were green and hideous to look at. But they were wearing uniforms and they were very striking in appearance! They were high stepping as they marched, in perfect formation, as if preparing for battle. I was transfixed and could only watch as this vision ran its course. I attempted to evaluate this vision as I viewed these demons, passing from left to right, when suddenly I heard extremely loud barking which seemed to snap me out of that spiritual realm. The barking was coming from my dog, which was in the backyard. Now as I began coming out of the vision, I turned my attention to my dog and his frantic barking.

I discovered him to be running back and forth along our backyard. He ran left to right looking up at the exact area where I had seen the demons in my vision. The next day I was watching the news on TV, and saw a broadcast where the army of North Korea had threatened

121

to initiate what would be considered an act that could lead to warfare and the deployment of nuclear arms.

The news segment showed the North Koreans: they were dressed in green uniforms, marching, high-stepping, in the same direction and formation as the demons in my vision. It was as if I was seeing the same vision repeated on TV, except that now I was viewing actual human beings in the natural. Denise and I prayed to the Lord using the protocol that was given us by Him. He answered our requests and informed us that the demons shown me through the gifting of the Holy Spirit were actually in those soldiers who were marching in that communist country footage broadcast on the news. We prayed for God's sovereign hand to maintain peace in all plans and situations concerning any impending violence in regards to the vision. Meanwhile, God was not slowing down. He was facilitating His plan for our lives in all directions. During this time we knew a woman whom I will call Jackie. She lived down the street from us. Jackie was a large strong woman who weighed in excess of 260 lbs. She was a vibrant grandmother of about 60 years of age.

She and her family had been living in the neighborhood even before we moved back in 1986. Jackie had a daughter who was in her late 30's to early 40's.

The daughter had three teenaged boys, but also a drug addiction and was in and out of jail. As is often the case with grandmothers, Jackie was instrumental in helping to raise those three boys. Jackie was a sweetheart, but had a tough, salty side as well. She could curse like a sailor. The word was that when she was young she used to win fights against men, bare-knuckle style. On most evenings after dark it was commonplace to hear Jackie's strong voice bellowing throughout the neighborhood, calling those boys to "Get your so and so's in this house right now!" She would walk the block to insure that her grandsons stayed out of trouble. Well, one day the Lord told Denise and I that He would soon "bring Jackie home."

He said she didn't have much time left. The Lord said that Denise would go to Jackie and tell her that she was to prepare herself. He said to tell her that God is Holy and that she had to begin cleaning up her speech, her heart, etc. Although we didn't know exactly how to convey this message to Jackie, we knew we had to be obedient to God's instructions. So we prayed that God would give Denise the words and Jackie the heart to receive them. We wondered how much time God would give Jackie before calling her home, a year, 2 years, 10 years?

After all, God's idea of a short span of time can be much different than our expectations. At that time we were afraid to even ask the Lord. Still, Denise found the courage to visit Jackie and tell her that God loved her and wanted to commune with her. She informed Jackie that God is so Holy that He can't look upon sinful behavior, so if Jackie wanted a relationship in the presence of the Lord, she had to try to clean up her language as God sought to cleanse her heart, in order to develop a friendship with her, and soon. Surprisingly, Jackie was agreeable, and said she would make the effort. In the next few days her conduct and demeanor began to change for the better.

We were even visited by a close friend of Jackie's who thanked us, whispering for us to please continue doing whatever Denise had done to calm Jackie down. The friend didn't know that it certainly wasn't us, but the power of God Himself.

A couple of days afterward, Jackie's daughter appeared at our door crying. She asked us to pray for her mom.

She said, "The doctors have discovered that my mother has inoperable cancer."

Denise and I just looked at her and each other. Curiously I asked her, "Did they say how long your mother has?"

In between tears she replied, "They give her 2 months."

As we stood in our doorway listening to Jackie's daughter, the Lord placed in Denise's heart to not only pray for Jackie, but for her daughter as well. In obedience we began praying for them both, right there in our

125

doorway. After the prayer was finished, the daughter tearfully left our house.

Denise and I looked at each other in wonderment. How could it be anything else but God that her daughter would come to us and ask us to pray for her mother?

The doctors had just discovered that she had inoperable cancer! Here was confirmation of what the Lord had told us just days earlier. Well, it didn't take two months for Jackie to pass. Jackie went from being a strong vibrant salty woman to passing away, and in the presence of the Lord, all within two weeks.

This word of wisdom God had given us in order to continue strengthening our faith in Him. He told us later that Jackie was now with Him in heaven.

When Jackie's daughter came to our door and was telling us about her mom, the Lord urged Denise to begin immediately praying for her daughter right then and there.

126

Well, as I said earlier, the daughter had a drug habit. Unbeknownst to Denise and me, the daughter was on her way to buy drugs when she came to our door.

After she left, she intended to meet her drug connection and score some drugs. I went to work and returned home later that day. Upon returning home from work, I noticed that the daughter's car had been involved in an accident and apparently had been towed to their front door. The car was obviously totaled. It looked as if it had been hit by a train. The front end was so damaged and the windshield smashed that one would assume that whoever was driving it at the time of the obvious accident or collision must certainly had been killed or at least severely injured.

Well, Denise and I read the newspaper that day and lo and behold…on the front page of the *West County Times* newspaper was an article with a large picture of Jackie's daughter's car. The car had in fact been hit by a train. Miraculously, Jackie's daughter walked away from the accident with one scratch on her clavicle.

It turns out that after she left our front door, she drove a 20 minutes distance to another neighborhood called *Parchester Village* to buy drugs. While she was driving across a railroad crossing, her car was struck by a train. The impact caused the car to turn at a precise angle, sparing her serious injury; while causing the seatbelt to activate. This was God's intervention, because we were later told by the daughter that prior to the day of the accident, the car's seat belt was broken and had not worked. That seat belt had been inoperable for years, until that day, 20 minutes after the Lord urged us to begin immediately praying for Jackie's daughter.

This was how the Lord was teaching Denise and me to diligently obey His commands. To procrastinate when God gives His commands is a form of disobedience. We have to always remember that God's time is always the best time.

CHAPTER TEN

PLACE THEM IN THE BUCKET

"As for Sarai your wife, you shall not call her name Sarai, but Sarah shall be her name." (Genesis 17:15)

One day, as Denise and I were communicating with the Lord through divine writing, He referred to her by a different name. The name turned out to be AnnaLisa. At first we wondered whom He was talking about. So we asked the Lord and He said that this was the new name by which Denise would be called. Denise happens to have a twin brother named Dennis.

The Lord said Denise was not the name that *He* had planned for my wife to have. He said that years ago when Denise and her twin brother were born, Denise's mother had not heeded the voice of the Lord when she named them. The Lord said that Denise and I were to take the necessary steps to effect a legal name change as soon as possible.

The Lord said to us, "Joel will do the research and facilitate your name change."

129

The Lord wanted this done ASAP. I didn't have any idea how I was to accomplish this. But one of the things I have learned in my walk with the Lord is that you do not have to know how to follow His commands, just willing to do as He commands.

God knows that some of the things He tells us aren't going to make sense to us or to others around us. But we have to be steadfast in our obedience to His commands.

The following couple of days, Denise and I were at church and one of the female members approached us, and for reasons unknown to us (but certainly known to God) she excitedly began to thoroughly explain to us the steps necessary for one to attain a legal name change in the State of California (Surprise!!). It was as if this woman had been programmed to approach us and deliver this information. In retrospect I know that is exactly what happened through the supernatural guidance of God.

In Isaiah 65:24, the Lord spoke the following words through His prophet,

"It shall come to pass that before they call I will answer; and while they are still speaking I will hear."

God knew what I needed and before I ever even asked Him, He sent someone with the answer. I gathered the information provided and proceeded to get the necessary applications in order to begin facilitating the name change. I was a little dismayed when I discovered that it would cost approximately $360; which at the time was about all we had in our bank account, give or take a few dollars.

Did this make sense to us that we were given instructions to change her name? No, not completely. Did we feel we could afford to spend that kind of money (our last) for a name change? Absolutely not! Let's be real...in the natural sense, it simply would not be a prudent move to up and spend your last dime to secure a legal name change.

Most rational people would say to do so would be foolish. Ah but the word of God says in 1 Corinthians 1:27 that *"God has chosen the foolish things of the world to put to shame the wise..."* So while Denise and I certainly didn't feel as if we had the money at the time, we were certain that God did. For all money belongs to God. In our walk with God we have come to realize that things don't always have to make sense to us, as long as it makes sense to God. That is really the deciding factor. That's what truly matters.

So Denise and I went to the county clerk's office. After filling out all of the application forms, securing Denise's records and social security card number, etc., I proceeded to wait in line for what seemed like an eternity. To my disappointment, when I reached the clerk's window she said their office would not accept credit or debit cards.

Wouldn't you know it, all I had on me at the time was my bank card. The woman looked at me demurely and informed me that there was a bank nearby, suggesting that I pay it a visit. With that I had no choice but to exit the window that I had waited so long to reach, and walked outside, searching for the bank. As I hurriedly exited the clerk's office looking for the bank, it began to rain.

I was becoming frustrated and thought, *"Great! Here I am getting drenched in the rain, looking to draw out the last of my money, in order to change my wife's name, and for what!?"* Then the Lord spoke to my heart. Who was it that was giving me instructions anyway? Who had sent angels to my wife and me? Who was guiding our lives? It was all God!

I realized that this was a test of obedience. The devil and his demons did not want us to accomplish the job that God had given us. I gathered myself, and determined to be obedient. I soon arrived at the bank and withdrew the money needed for the name change. Finally, I arrived once again at the clerk's window (*"Heeeee's Baaack!! Take that, Satan!"* I thought). Denise's name was officially and legally changed to AnnaLisa that day. Praise God! The devil's scheme had been thwarted. God's will had been done.

133

It's interesting to note that neither AnnaLisa nor I had any inclination to have her name changed prior to God instructing us to do so. But what is uncanny is that we discovered later that the name *AnnaLisa* means *"grace, favor, consecrated and oath of God."* On the other hand, the name *Denise* means *lover of wine*, or *wine goddess*. Is it a coincidence that both of AnnaLisa's parents were alcoholics, as well as two of her siblings? I think not.

I know that through Jesus' saving grace and limitless love and power, yokes and strongholds are broken supernaturally. God was reclaiming His daughter.

No longer would she wear the clothes of sin and unrighteousness. The Lord was adorning her with a wardrobe of righteousness, and it included a name change as well.

As our walk with God deepened, AnnaLisa and I would learn that many times, being obedient to the Lord comes with unforeseen challenges and sacrifices. For instance, we quickly discovered that not everyone was happy about the name change. Most were okay with it. But for some, it was all right if Denise wanted to call herself AnnaLisa, but it was an entirely different matter when *they* were expected to address her by that name.

Some people were direct enough to say, "You'll always be Denise to me," or, "I like Denise, so I'll call you Denise." Here it was, Denise's right to change her name even if the Lord had *not* commanded her, but people were behaving as if it was their right to address her any way they pleased. One day, after having explained to certain relatives about what God had commanded us to do with changing her name, AnnaLisa happened to place a telephone call to some of her close relatives in Chicago.

The telephone conversation went as follows: "Hello, this is AnnaLisa."

The relative responded with, "I don't know any AnnaLisa, but I do have a sister named Denise," and hung up the phone.

135

This same relative after some time, eventually accepted AnnaLisa's call, but insisted that God had not instructed us to facilitate the name change. The sad part was that this relative was at least a 30-year Christ follower, and instead of embracing AnnaLisa and rejoicing in this marvelous move of God, jealousy and envy had found their place in her heart (and also maybe a bit of unbelief).

She simply couldn't understand why God was revealing Himself to AnnaLisa and me in such dramatic ways. One relative who did graciously accept AnnaLisa's name was her twin brother Dennis. Dennis was always somewhat of a comedian and said he only had one question, and that question was, "If God is changing your name, does that mean I have to change mine as well?"

At first I thought he was serious, and then I saw his wide grin and laughter. He admitted that he was joking. Dennis then expressed his opinion saying that the name AnnaLisa struck him as being a very beautiful name. Around this same time, Dennis expressed to

AnnaLisa that he wished he could find the wife of his dreams.

AnnaLisa, being led by God's Holy Spirit, advised Dennis that she would pray that God would send His choice for a wife for Dennis.

As always, God heard AnnaLisa's prayers. It had been years since Dennis had even entertained in his mind the prospect of entering into a new relationship. Now, miraculously only 5-7 days after the prayer, Dennis was attending church serving as an usher when he was approached by a beautiful woman who struck up a conversation with him.

The woman said her name was Simone and asked if she could use his pen. Dennis obliged and a conversation ensued. Somewhere in their conversing, Simone told Dennis that she had been noticing him for quite some time and was actually interested in meeting him. Dennis and Simone discovered that they had quite a bit in common, and the two became friends. Dennis couldn't wait to tell his twin AnnaLisa about what was happening in his life.

AnnaLisa was not surprised however, because God had said that He sent Simone to Dennis. Still some of Dennis' family members were skeptical, and not only cautioned Dennis, but also attempted to dissuade him from diving into the relationship. Amazingly, the same people who doubted the relationship would eventually come to see beyond a shadow of a doubt that this courtship was clearly sanctioned and arranged by God Himself.

It turned out that years ago, as a young man, Dennis had served as an Airborne Ranger in the U.S. Army. Surprisingly, Simone also served in the Army (no, not as a Ranger, but as a nurse). And while Dennis and Simone did not serve during the exact same time span due to their age differences when enlisting, they both would come to discover that each had served at Fort Bragg, North Carolina.

Dennis happened to be married at the time. So neither he, nor Simone had any knowledge of the other during that time. Still their lives had followed the same distinct paths; from Chicago to membership in the same branch of service in the Army, to Fort Bragg, North Carolina and back; then to become members of the same church in Indiana, where God was saying… "It's time!"

So powerful was their relationship that they were engaged within a few weeks. Their lives seem to fit together like two puzzle pieces, each possessing exactly what was needed by the other in order to make a secure connection as one. Dennis and Simone's individual strengths and weaknesses balanced each other out. Where Dennis had been searching for a mate on his own during his early years, neither of his marriages lasted. Yet Simone had never married, petitioning God that she would do so only if and when God provided the man for her. In other areas where Simone may have been less detail oriented, Dennis' perfectionism and attention to detail became an asset. Their courtship emerged as an example of godliness.

The two were able to honor God's statues regarding celibacy until their marriage, approximately one year after their initial meeting. Since that time, God has prospered them physically, mentally, economically and of course spiritually because of their continued obedience to God's calling. He has blessed them in ministry at their church.

God knows the hearts of His people. Even though Dennis was not walking with the Lord as he should have in the beginning. God knew all along that Dennis would accept the news about his sister's name change. Only God can know what favor and eternal blessing will be the result of the faith and obedience displayed by Dennis and Simone, which all began with Dennis humbly receiving the news that it was indeed God who was changing his twin sister's name to AnnaLisa.

This is why we as Christ followers must continually search the word of God without reservation. God is not a respecter of persons, as Peter mentions in Acts 10:34-35. The Lord shows no partiality, and seeks

140

to use those who will humbly obey Him. We must continually examine and digest God's word, as the bible instructs in 2 Tim 2:15. We will then be less inclined to be led away due to our fleshly desires and emotions (jealousy and envy), which can cause us to depart from biblical teaching. How true it is that we must all take careful steps to, *"Let this mind be in us which was also in Christ Jesus,"* as mentioned in Philippians 2:5.

Now just prior to the Lord directing us to effect the name change, AnnaLisa and I were attending a nearby church; for the Lord had spoken to us by again manifesting Himself in AnnaLisa and taking over her body. He told me that we were to attend a church near our home. The Lord gave us the name of the church, and although I had previously repented my sins to Him, He told me that from time to time, I would remember other past sins for which I may not have remembered and thus, not formally repented of those sins. He told me to write them down and to repent to Him each time one of these sins came to my remembrance.

141

The Lord instructed me to then take my list of sins to this church and give them to His servant at that church. The Lord said that the pastor of this church was the humble servant of which He spoke. I did exactly as I was told. My wife and I obediently arrived at the church and were seated in the balcony. To my surprise, the pastor had placed a huge 8-10 foot tall cross on the platform with a bucket at the base of the cross.

The pastor stands up, appearing to be looking directly up at my wife and me and said, "If there is anyone here who needs to write down his sins and bring them to me, please do so. Place them in this bucket and I will take them home and burn them." I was flabbergasted! He had spoken nearly the exact same words and given the same directions the Lord had given to my wife and me only a few hours earlier.

We waited on the Lord and eventually joined the church, but not before the Lord had given us the go ahead to do so. After following God's instructions to join this church, God eventually told us that we would join the choir. As if on cue, a few days later, the choir director asked us to join the choir. Later, the Lord informed us to prepare to join the worship team. Again, just days afterward we got the word from God, the choir director called us in to ask when we would join the worship team. AnnaLisa and I continued to dutifully serve the Lord, complying with His orders whether we understood or not. I must add that AnnaLisa and I still comply with God's commands wholeheartedly to this day. Obedience is important if one is to continually hear from God and properly discern His voice.

Now AnnaLisa and I had consistently received voice training for the 20 or so years of singing R&B music prior to our meeting the Lord. But the Lord told us through divine writing that we would begin receiving vocal training from a specific anointed minister of music (First Lady Hunter) and we did. Mrs. Hunter's husband is Pastor Hunter. We became fast friends and brothers/sisters in Christ and remain so today.

I often pondered what exactly the Lord meant when He said that my wife and I would no longer sing

143

R&B music, but instead would sing gospel/inspirational music. Of course I did not know even one standard hymn or Christian song back in 2004. Quite frankly, prior to 2004 I didn't care for gospel music at all.

But let me tell you what God did; I was asleep a few days after the "bedroom meeting with Jesus." Again, it was in the wee hours of the morning when I heard lyrics of a song playing in my head saying, *God is the power and the glory, and if you turn to Him, you won't have to worry.* I woke up and wondered, "What's going on? What song is that? *Whose* song is that?" It was as if I knew this song, but I couldn't know it because I didn't know any gospel or Christian songs. So after a few minutes of trying to figure out this very distinct tune and lyrics, sleep overtook me and again, I was out.

It must have been seconds later that the song began again…this time with more lyrics, *God is the power and the glory. And if you turn to Him, you won't have to worry. So why are you waiting, stop hesitating. God is the power and the glory.* I sat up in bed, my eyes wide open. The tune was reverberating in my head. It wouldn't let me sleep. I could clearly hear the melody, the base guitar, the lead guitar, drums, etc.

I climbed out of bed and sat at the kitchen table. I retrieved a pen and paper and availed myself to the Lord as His vessel. The words to the song *God is the Power* were soon completed. After that song, there were many others that the Lord sent me, including *Hold on, God's Wrath, Nobody but Jesus,* and many more. Many of them have simply come as I was sleeping or just driving or walking along and then, Boom!!

A song begins to take shape. It was shortly after receiving the first tune in my sleep that God instructed AnnaLisa and me that we would enroll in a local community college to study the music and songwriting business.

We immediately complied with the Lord's instructions. To our surprise (but again, not to God's surprise) when we entered the class, we learned that the instructor happened to be a well-known entertainment attorney who had worked in the secular world with the likes of *Earth, Wind & Fire* and *Michael Jackson.*

He began teaching us how to get our music copyrighted and published. The Lord told us that we would soon join ASCAP as songwriters and recording artists.

It was soon done. Although we had little or no knowledge of the business end of gospel music, God's divine hand was upon us and guiding us step by step.

CHAPTER ELEVEN

WHAT WILL THEY THINK OF US?

"Sing to the Lord a new song and His praise to the end of the earth." (Isaiah 42:10)

The songs were coming fast and furiously. I had scraps of paper with lyrics written on them all over the house. My head was a rolodex of lyrics, tunes, and scriptures. God had programmed my mind so that when I read His word, the scriptures seemed to jump out at me with meaning and understanding. I easily found the bible to be God's Holy word, infiltrating my senses.

AnnaLisa and I both absolutely relished reading the bible. So we were constantly writing songs sent to us in the spirit, *by* the Spirit. The Lord eventually sent us to an anointed producer, musician, and man of God named David Decuir, and told us that David would assist us in having our first original gospel CD produced. Soon afterwards, we had completed our first CD entitled *Spiritual Warfare.* It was a collection of 10 original gospel tunes, each with its own powerful message from

God. Each song had its own individual genre, style, and flavor.

In the following days the Lord told AnnaLisa and I that we would be traveling to South Africa on a missionary assignment. Neither I nor AnnaLisa knew a thing about South Africa or traveling to the continent. I'm not even sure if we wanted to go there.

However, we knew that if God said it, we had to do it. We are and were His vessels. It turned out - of course - that God arranged our every move. He put a wonderful pastor named Tommie Gilbert in my path. Pastor Gilbert and I had worked as police officers long before the Lord called me. Since that time, Tommie was no longer in law enforcement and had started his own church. On one occasion, Pastor Gilbert happened to hear our *Spiritual Warfare* CD.

Upon hearing it, he said, "You and AnnaLisa must come to South Africa with us next year and minister to the people there." He said, "They need to hear this word."

AnnaLisa and I try never to promise anything except that we will ask the Lord that His will be done in our lives. So we promised Tommie that we would pray about it. We did, and the Lord gave confirmation that we would indeed go to South Africa.

"Go therefore and make disciples of all the nations, baptizing them in the name of the Father and of the Son and of the Holy Spirit, teaching them to observe all things that I have commanded you, and lo, I am with you always, even to the end of the age." Amen. (Matthew 28:19 & 20)

Well now that the Lord had said that we would go to South Africa, we wondered how this was to take place. AnnaLisa and I were not pastors or even ordained ministers at that time. We were simply children of God trying to follow His every word. Two people God had chosen before the foundation of the world to be His vessels. We were a far cry from being experienced missionaries. So we waited for the Lord to instruct us on how this mission assignment to South Africa was to be accomplished.

Pastor Gilbert had said that he would get the paperwork started. Pastor Gilbert was affiliated with *Faith Missions International.* It was headed by Bishop Herman Tinsley and his wife Pastor Patrice Tinsley, who happened to be Pastor Gilbert's older sibling. This group had been doing wonderful missionary work in South Africa for at least 14 years at the time. During that period they had fed and clothed the poor, taught pastors, hosted conferences, and planted schools for the kingdom of God.

AnnaLisa and I had no knowledge about how anything was to take place, but as I always say, you don't have to know how; you just have to know God, and be obedient to Him. God was about to lay out His plan for us to travel and minister in South Africa. We learned that we would need $10,200 for AnnaLisa and me to travel round trip, with room and board, to South Africa. Well, $10,200 may as well have been 10 million dollars! I was

150

the only one working and we were living paycheck-to-paycheck, juggling bills as needed. We were about to learn that God's ways are much higher than our ways (as it says in Isa 55:8-9). It turns out that this was the time that AnnaLisa and I had just completed our first gospel CD, *Spiritual Warfare*. The Lord instructed us that we would hold a gospel concert at our church. He said we would name the event *A Celebration of Faith*. God said He would send competent people our way to facilitate this.

Now AnnaLisa and I knew nothing about hosting or producing a concert event, but we didn't have to. The Lord took the reins and sent the right people our way. He sent gifted local gospel artists such as the Hartfield Brothers, Minister Ronnie Mills, and others to glorify the name of the Lord in song and dance. The production crew was headed up by Mark Johnson. We received advertising assistance, interviews, and airplay from top radio personalities such as Ms. Monika Kelly of KNDL Radio and the legendary Mr. Emmit Powell of KPFA Radio.

151

The two-hour event was such a success that in one night we had made enough proceeds to cover the cost of the South Africa assignment. At the time we were members of a church that seated approximately 1400 people. That CD release was the first time in that church's history that the sanctuary had been filled to near capacity. That night the Spirit of the Lord fell heavily in that church. His anointing was on each artist and servant who had said "yes" to use their gifts and talents that night for the Lord. Funding for God's assignment was pouring in.

Over the next day, more proceeds came in. The final total was not only adequate to meet the $10,200 needed, but as the bible scripture mentions it "ran over into our bosoms," the final tally was in excess of $12,000. God had blessed us to witness that He can indeed do *exceedingly and abundantly greater than we could ever ask or imagine.* (Ephesians 3:20)

We were able to bless the church and now would be able to be a blessing to our brothers and sisters abroad. With that we were given the final go ahead to prepare for

South Africa. AnnaLisa and I were soon introduced to the eight-man crew that would be traveling together to do God's work in South Africa. The crew so far consisted of Bishop Herman Tinsley, his wife Pastor Patrice Tinsley, Pastor Tommie Gilbert, Minister/Dr. Willie Dye, Minister Linda Cole, Bishop/Dr. Les Johnson, AnnaLisa and I. We were so excited about this assignment. Certainly AnnaLisa and I didn't know what to expect. We just wanted to be diligent in doing the work of the Lord. Our part of the mission's ministry would be to witness and minister to all through music and testimony. Just prior to going to South Africa we received startling news that Pastor Tommie Gilbert had suffered a fatal heart attack.

Tommie had been a life long martial arts champion prior to becoming a preacher, and he had founded the *Best In The West* martial arts club in San Leandro, CA. There he had trained some of the most proficient martial artists and police officers in the Bay Area of California. Even with his work in the pulpit, Tommie still found time to instruct, helping to guide young men and women in and out of the walls of the church. It was during a training session that the Lord called him home. The night brother Tommie went home, AnnaLisa and I received a divine message from the Lord concerning Pastor Gilbert saying,

"He lives, he lives, he lives…" Thinking of (John 11:25-26) *He who believes in Me though he dies, shall live: and he who lives and believes in Me shall never die.*

I knew my brother had passed on from this natural realm into God's heavenly realm and would live forevermore with the Lord. The Lord told us that Tommie had served his purpose, and was called home. The baton had been handed off to AnnaLisa and me. Now it was on to South Africa.

We were warmly welcomed in South Africa and would minister in Johannesburg and Sashanguve, among other places. It was during our assignment in South Africa that we got to know Bishop Les Johnson, a wonderful man of God who was part of the team, along with the Faith Missions team.

As we spent time together giving our testimonies, the presence of God would at times be so strong that all would feel the hand of God upon us. I noticed these men of God both American and South African addressing me as "Pastor." I repeatedly attempted to correct them, telling them that I was not a pastor, but to no avail. They would only smile, and some would insist "But you *are* a pastor." One evening the Lord told AnnaLisa and me that I was to get up the next morning at 8:00AM and go to Bishop Tinsley's room and tell him that the Lord said for him and Bishop Johnson to ordain AnnaLisa and me as ministers.

Of course, this caught us by surprise. I'm not the type of person to be presumptuous, or assuming when it comes to dealing with people, especially when I do not know them very well. But what could I do but say, "Yes, Lord." Still, I wrestled that night with the thought of what I had to do come morning at 8:00AM. Who was I to recommend that my wife and I be ordained as ministers?

I thought to myself, "*What will they think of us?*"

8:00AM came swiftly. Obediently I went to Bishop Tinsley's room and knocked on the door. "Come in," he replied.

I sheepishly entered, observing that the Bishop was still relaxed in bed with his arms outstretched and hands behind his head.

"Good morning, Joel."

"Good morning, Bishop," I said as I sought the proper words to preface my reason for coming to his room.

"Bishop Tinsley, I know you've seen how the Lord communicates with AnnaLisa and me...how we get messages from Him....right?" Bishop Tinsley nodded affirmatively, and I continued,

"How we are obedient to His instructions, right?"

156

Bishop Tinsley responded, "Yes, Joel."

I then explained that… "Well, Bishop, last night the Lord told AnnaLisa and me that I was to come here this morning at 8:00AM, before group prayer, and inform you that you and Bishop Johnson would ordain AnnaLisa and I as ministers of God."

I then produced the paper with the divine message written just as the Lord had dictated it to us.

I said, "I have it written here just as the Lord gave it to us. May I read it to you?" The Bishop told me to go ahead. I read it word for word to the Bishop. The message mentioned that the Lord had placed my wife and me with these two *mighty men of God* for a reason, and that they would facilitate the ordination upon our return to the U.S. from the South African missionary assignment.

There, I had said it! What a difficult thing to do. It reminded me of when I was a youngster in Chicago and my mother would line us up before school in the winter months and make us take cod liver oil. I would hold my

157

breath and swallow, quickly inhaling and exhaling after it was down. That's sort of the way I felt at that moment in front of Bishop Tinsley. I stood there unsure of what the Bishop's reaction would be to what I had just said. Silence!

Bishop Tinsley propped himself up on his elbow attentively staring at me.

He then broke the silence and said, "The Lord gave you that message?" I thought to myself, *"Oh boy, here goes. He's going to think I made this up. Denise and I will be thrown out and put on the next plane back to America."*

But the devil is a liar! I had told the truth. So, in spite of my fears, I answered Bishop Tinsley's question truthfully and said,

"Yes, Bishop, the Lord gave us that message."

What happened next was so amazing that I truly came to understand the sovereign, omniscience of the

God we serve. When I stood on the word of God, Bishop Tinsley began to smile, first to himself, and then loudly chuckling.

He said "Joel, last night the Lord gave us (meaning Bishop Johnson and him) a message as well, telling us that we needed to ordain the both of you. We just didn't know how to tell you guys. We didn't know if you would accept it or not."

The Bishop produced a piece of paper with a message corroborating what he had told me. He was still laughing and shaking his head, obviously as relieved as I was. I stood there numb and thanked Bishop Tinsley.

As I turned to leave the room he asked me,

"Joel, the Lord called me a mighty man of God you say?"

I turned to him, "Yes, sir."

Bishop Tinsley just smiled.

He said, "I've got to call Bishop Johnson now."

"Yes, sir," I said.

As I left the room, tears filled my eyes as they do now.

I'm hearing the song *How great is our God...sing with me...how great is our God...all will see...how great...how great...is our God.*

AnnaLisa and I returned from that mission assignment with a better understanding of what God had been saying to us. We were learning that OJT (On the Job Training) with God comes quickly and succinctly depending on His purpose for your life. God had afforded us the opportunity to see His miraculous hand moving in so many ways. He also provided us with an opportunity to minister His word overseas, both through testimony and song. Each time, the Lord would go before us, setting the atmosphere and breaking up the fallow ground. The recipients were hungry and hopeful for the word of God.

WHAT WILL THEY THINK OF US?

The Lord was preparing us. Prior to leaving the U.S. for South Africa, a brother at our church named Wayne Perrault had given AnnaLisa and I a book about a well-known man of God named Reinhart Bonke.

He had trail blazed in South Africa and brought countless souls to Christ, hundreds of thousands I was told. While in South Africa AnnaLisa and I met and spent time with a woman named Paulina. She was once a notorious witch in South Africa who had been delivered and saved and brought to salvation through Jesus Christ.

AnnaLisa and I learned later, through reading Mr. Bonke's book, that Paulina (now regarded as Apostle Paulina) had received Jesus through meeting brother Bonke. AnnaLisa and I knew that our assignment there served as an introduction of sorts in order to prep us for what God had in store for our life's work, both at home and abroad.

"And they overcame him by the blood of the Lamb and the word of their testimony." (Revelation 12:11a)

161

When we returned to the U.S. and our home church, we were bursting at the seams. We were excited, wanting to share the good news in relation to what God had revealed to us during our time in South Africa. We wanted to share with the congregation the miraculous events that had transpired.

We hoped to be able to edify the church that it might grow in faith and obedience to God in order to realize all that He has for His children. But after returning home we found the church to be business as usual. We learned that some of the leaders in the church were uncomfortable with our missionary assignment to South Africa. Here it was that basically for most of our lives, AnnaLisa and I had been about as far away from Christ as two people could be; but God chose to scoop us up, clean us up, and then raise us up.

It was God who had begun teaching us, then sending us out on the road to do His will, and with dramatic results. While most in our church applauded the moves of God in our lives, as we gave Him all the glory;

there were some who outright rejected having anything positive to do with, or say about what God was doing in our lives.

But the Lord reminded us of Rom 8:28,

"All things work together for good to those who love God; to those who are the called according to His purpose."

The Lord instructed us to pray for those in the church who may have hardness of hearts. We complied, praying fervently and continued to serve the Lord with even more vigor and determination.

AnnaLisa and I were being taught by the Holy Spirit of God. We were learning more about God as we learned more about His word. We were learning valuable lessons about the church in general, and one important lesson was that churches many times become confused and wind up doing church instead of being the church. In so doing, many church folks may read daily devotions and scriptures, show up in church on Sunday, pay their tithes, and even praise the Lord.

But if one neglects to develop a true hunger and a thirst for the Lord and all He stands for…if one refuses to proclaim the Good News; and make an effort each day striving to become truly changed and transformed for God's purpose, one's relationship with Christ is superficial, or *surface level* at best.

CHAPTER TWELVE

AN OVERSIZED SARDINE

It was about one year later that AnnaLisa and I received communication from a pastor in Bapatla, India named L. Vinay Kumar. He had been given a revelation that we were to come to India and minister to the people of his country. Of course, AnnaLisa and I received what pastor Kumar told us; however, we politely informed the pastor that we move only when God directs us through confirmation.

We assured him that we would travel anywhere in the world, but only upon hearing from God directly and in this case we would have to await confirmation from God.

Very shortly thereafter the Lord spoke to AnnaLisa and I both and detailed that we would indeed travel to Southern India to preach His word. The Lord then gave us a brief history of India through programs and literature. By this I mean that God began to inundate AnnaLisa and I with information about the people and

165

customs of India. The Lord started bringing in both people from the country of India, as well as experienced missionaries to assist us in preparation for our upcoming assignment in India. On one occasion, two or three missionaries traveled to our church and sought out AnnaLisa and myself in order to offer their assistance should we require it of them. It was quite amazing but we barely had to do much at all in order to facilitate traveling to India. The Lord told us to tell the prayer warriors and others in our church that we would soon travel to India for an assignment.

We obeyed His every command. In short order we had our tickets for travel to India as well as enough finances both to sustain us during the India assignment, as well as to provide assistance for pastor Kumar and his people. Of course this was not met without opposition from Satan and his demons.

Just as the Lord was allowing things to progress ever so smoothly concerning our preparing to leave for India, AnnaLisa and I found that the pastorate and leadership at our home church were staunchly against supporting us in any way on our quest! At one point our pastor disparaged the pastor from India, insinuating in error that this pastor worshipped other gods and idols, and possibly snakes. This was after our pastor had viewed a picture of the pastor from India holding what appeared to him to be a replica of a snake, but was in fact only a makeshift microphone wrapped in a handkerchief for noise reduction.

But the Lord was gracious, God reasoned with AnnaLisa and me that if this were indeed the case (that if these Indians really did worship snakes and other gods), what better reason for us to go and bring the Good News to these "lost" people? But of course this was not the case, at least not with the pastors we would encounter. It was only a move of the enemy through spiritual warfare attempting to keep AnnaLisa and I from going to India, by blinding the eyes of the church leadership where we served.

But that is the thing about spiritual warfare; as in physical warfare, sometimes you've got to press your way through spirits of opposition, doubt, and fear.

The Lord continued to guide us, insisting that instead of becoming anxious, AnnaLisa and I were to continue praying for our brothers/sisters who were caught up in fear, and uncertainty.

"Finally my brethren, be strong in the Lord and the power of His might. Put on the whole amour of God that you may be able to stand against the wiles of the devil." (Ephesians 6:10-11)

Our travel date was soon upon us. My wife and I were scheduled to depart for India the following day. We went to the bank to secure the appropriate finances for living expenses while in India, as well as financial assistance for the people of India.

When I gave the teller my bank information, seeking to withdraw the funds from my account, the teller looked puzzled and said, "Mr. Jones, it seems that your account is overdrawn."

I knew that couldn't be possible, for AnnaLisa and I had been careful not to disturb anything in the account, so as not to hamper the work God had for us in India. To make matters worse, the amount of money that was drawn out was much more than we even had in the account in the first place!

It turned out that the bank had authorized purchases of several tickets to Hawaii to be taken from our account. We soon learned that the tickets were printed up in Oklahoma of all places.

Therefore I said,

"This can't be, we don't even have that much money in our account, and why would I purchase tickets to Hawaii on succeeding days…and from Oklahoma when we live in California?" It made no sense at all.

The teller said, "We can do a fraud check and restore the funds to your account within 7 days."

That was the tip-off. Both AnnaLisa and I knew that this was no more than a last ditch effort by the devil to keep us from going to India. Here we were set to depart to India the following morning and Satan was trying to block our travel. All the money we had to our name was in my front pocket. I had about $119 in my pocket.

So when that teller said,

"We can restore your funds within 7 days."

I said, "Ma'am we don't have seven days. We can't even wait seven hours. Money or no money, we are leaving to India tomorrow morning."

I looked at AnnaLisa, who was already verbally praying against this evil (Oh, how God answers true prayer warriors!).

By now you can guess what happened. God heard our prayers!! That bank office began moving with quickness I've never seen. They summoned the manager, and not only did they recover our funds, but they provided us a credit amount which gave us a financial cushion in *excess* of the amount we had originally.

AnnaLisa excitedly said, "Look at God!!"

Again, He had taken what Satan intended as evil to bring out good for His children.

Well, AnnaLisa and I were more determined than ever to follow God's instructions, doing our part to spread the Gospel of Christ to the uttermost areas of the world, in this case India.

We knew this would be difficult for us, because unlike the assignment in South Africa where we had an entourage of experienced missionaries accompanying us, the Lord was not sending anyone else to accompany us to India.

171

It was as if God had allowed us to cut our teeth in South Africa; although, it was dangerous as well as a hardship of sorts, through it all AnnaLisa and I had been paired with a team of experienced American men and women of God. They knew what to expect on the journey in Africa, even though we didn't. So in that respect we were somewhat prepared collectively in our own minds concerning uncertainties that might arise.

The India trek would prove to be entirely different. I would in essence be taking my wife into a very dark and dangerous country, at the request of the voice of the Lord. No one else!! No group or support system of people with which to travel and direct us. As I said earlier, our home church pastorate leadership had taken a *hands off* stance regarding assisting us in any fashion concerning our assignment from God. But our family members (saved and unsaved), as well as long time Christ followers were also questioning the logic in our decision to go to India. People would look at us as if to say, "Are you CRAZY?"

This only served to challenge us, to fuel our fire. We knew that it would be next to insane for a married couple such as AnnaLisa and me to risk our lives and go thousands of miles across the world to India and face danger and possibly death on the instructions received in the spirit.

We couldn't feasibly plan this with any logical reasoning or explaining. All the cards were stacked against us. We had no support, save for a few dutiful prayer warriors staying on their knees and faces, praying on our behalf. We knew that in order for this assignment to transpire and be completed successfully, it would have to come from the mighty hand of God. Of course it would. Turns out that was exactly the way God planned it. God would not only make it happen, but He would be with us, guiding us every step of the way.

We arrived in India in the wee hours of the morning, about 2:30AM India time. Upon arrival inside of the small airport, we immediately noticed the air to be extremely humid. As we stepped into the airport corridor

173

the heat was almost overwhelming. It was at least 110 degrees at two in the morning. AnnaLisa and I busily headed toward baggage claim. Obviously we stood out as outsiders.

Back in America, I would not appear as noticeable, even with my shaved head and husky build. There are many large bald men in America. Oh, but not in India. It seems that I was the only truly large, bald man I ever saw while there. People immediately started approaching us as we retrieved our baggage. Although they were speaking in their native language, we soon deduced that they were asking if we needed a ride or transportation.

Some would make gestures and presumptuously grab at our bags as if to say,

"I will carry that for you," *without your permission.*

Immediately my police instincts kicked in.

174

I politely, yet sternly offered,

"No, thank you," while shaking my head along with the wave of a hand dismissing their offers.

Certainly the word of God instructs us to be as *wise as serpents, yet harmless as doves* (Matthew 10:16b).

I quickly discerned that it was certainly the time to be wise. I recognized that my wife and I might as well have had an American dollar bill sign emblazoned on our chests (Ka-ching!).

"*Not today,*" I thought.

We continued briskly walking through the airport and reached customs. At customs the officials eyed us as curiously as we also eyed them. I had heard all the stories about how officials in some countries will typically harass visitors in efforts to derive pay-offs. But each time the devil brought up these thoughts, God's peace seemed to follow. The questions were fairly standard and no issues arose.

Finally, we were cleared to exit the airport (Thank You, Jesus!).

We walked along a long corridor separated by a gate. On our side of the corridor (the left side) was the airport area. On the opposite side (the right side) was the true country of India. People were packed against this fence that seemed to be at least a block long. Hundreds of Indian people lined the fence area. AnnaLisa and I could only assume that they had come to the airport to meet people arriving in the country. Many slender to medium built Indians (mostly men) were calling out to their arriving parties.

Many held signs in hand in order for arriving parties to locate them. I found myself wondering how my wife and I would recognize Pastor Kumar. It was such a large sea of humanity. But as always, God is faithful. As I surveyed the fence area, I locked eyes with a small man

176

wildly gesturing and calling out to AnnaLisa and me. I recognized him to be Pastor Kumar.

He was still on the opposite side of the fence. So not wanting to lose him in the crowd, we kept our eyes on each other until we were able to reach him outside of the airport. Pastor Kumar came up to us. He was smiling excitedly, and shaking our hands. AnnaLisa drew him to her and gave him a warm, holy hug (which has been her custom ever since we became saved). We exchanged pleasantries and were led toward a waiting van and driver.

Again, I was amazed at the sweltering heat. Here it was two in the morning and I felt as if I was in midday Miami. AnnaLisa and I noticed that along the sidewalks across the streets that surrounded the airport, were hundreds of people lying down asleep. It looked like a massive sleep-in of some sort. I assumed that these were indigent people who needed a safe place to sleep and in efforts to catch a breeze in this brutal heat, they decided the airport would be the safest place.

177

There were certainly plenty of local armed personnel on hand. But AnnaLisa and I discovered later during our assignment in India, that entire families (who actually have homes) could be seen all sleeping outdoors in the open air just to catch a breeze. We soon reached the van. I was sweating profusely by then. Pastor Kumar repeatedly asked me if I was okay. I assured him that I was one to sweat easily, and I was fine. Still, my sweat jets would be working overtime in India; such was the humidity. So, I had already reasoned that I would count it all joy, and was seldom seen in India without a sweat towel in hand. Pastor Kumar introduced us to another Indian gentleman who apparently was an associate pastor.

We greeted each other and each of the men began loading our bags onto the van. AnnaLisa and I boarded, sitting in the back seat of the vehicle. Pastor Kumar and his assistant climbed in front, and we were off. They drove us to a hotel where AnnaLisa and I were to spend the first night. It was a very dark and dank hotel in a very rundown part of the city. There was trash strewn about in front of the building. The clerk was asleep (indoors this time). Pastor Kumar woke him and we received a room for the night. Once we were able to be alone in our room, reality seemed to set in.

Here we were, thousands of miles away from home. We were staying in a seedy hotel in a part of India where who knows what goes on. We had no idea what people were saying when speaking to us. The devil was whispering in our ears that there was danger all around us (anyone could break into our room, which by the way didn't appear secure at all, and rob us at gunpoint or knifepoint). We had no assurance of anything, except one thing, and that was that the Lord was with us. Whenever we felt ourselves becoming anxious, God would reassure us that He was with us, right there in our room, or wherever we were.

Let me tell you how good God is in caring for His children. *Long before you can ever even think of making plans, God has already arranged things and put people in place for you.* Before AnnaLisa and I had left the U.S.

for India, there was a pastor who heard our testimony and learned that we were about to go on a missionary assignment to India. He gave us the phone number of a missionary named Ursula Bowman. This pastor said he believed that Ms. Bowman was traveling to India as well, and felt that we should call her. He said his reason for recommending that we contact her was because he was sure that she was the only person he had ever met who followed God's leading as completely as my wife and I. Apparently she was truly led by the Spirit. According to the pastor, Sister Bowman was a Christian woman who had upped and left her professional career in social work, sold her house and embarked on her new career as a missionary for the Lord.

Since that time, Sister Ursula had traveled extensively across the world, alone. She was typically stationed in extremely dangerous areas doing God's work, with God being her only resource. The word was that she was a single American female who lived alone in India. After praying to the Lord and getting an affirmative response, we contacted her. Sure enough, Sister Ursula said that she would try to meet with us after we arrived in the country. Well, it turned out that not only did we meet her in India, but she stayed with Pastor AnnaLisa and I for a few days. During that time, we were lodging in the home of Pastor Kumar who was so gracious in housing the three of us. He even extended the sleeping quarters of his family, as well as his own to ensure that we were taken care of (may God continue to bless him 10 fold).

Sister Ursula accompanied us for a few days as we ministered in various villages. On one occasion, as we were ministering in a certain sanctuary; a demon possessed woman rushed the platform area, hissing inaudible sounds as her tongue darted in and out of her mouth like a reptile. Sister Ursula didn't miss a beat, but deftly stepped in front of the woman and rebuked the demonic spirit in the name of Jesus while grasping this woman's face. The woman slunk to the ground, and when she recovered she fled the building. She returned later only to stand quietly outside peering into the window as God's word continued to go forth through the three of us.

181

Obviously the Lord had placed Ursula with us in order to assist us as we went about our training as missionaries. After a few days we parted company, as Sister Ursula had to return to her primary assignment. We all embraced as she said, "I think you guys can handle it from here." Of course she knew we could as long as we had the Lord with us. Our friendship with Sister Ursula is of course, ongoing. As I said before, God gives you what you need when you need it, and she was indeed a godsend.

We learned that this was only the beginning in our faith walk in India. During our assignment in India, there came a time when Pastor Kumar told AnnaLisa and I that we all would need to travel to a city where we would minister the word of God. The people of that area were practicing other religions, including Hinduism. Apparently they worshipped many gods. AnnaLisa and I couldn't wait to introduce them to the One True God, who is Jesus Christ.

Pastor Kumar explained that we would need to travel eight hours by rail, and then at least four hours by car. Keep in mind that this came after about a 20-hour plane ride from the U.S. to India. Still, the joy of the Lord and doing His will was our strength. Pastor Kumar insisted he had already made provisions and that everything was in order for the train excursion.

So AnnaLisa and I arrived at the train station with Pastor Kumar. There were not many people at the station, a man here, a couple of women there. I remember seeing what appeared to be a group of family members with a couple of young teenagers meandering about. AnnaLisa and I were seated waiting for the train. Nothing seemed out of the ordinary. I noticed that the station was set up where patrons waiting to board a train sat on either side of two sets of train tracks. In other words, there was a platform where passengers could sit and await their train.

The platform was situated next to the train tracks. Approximately 20-30 feet further across was another platform where one could wait for a train going in the opposite direction. Each platform was situated about 3-4

183

feet higher than the train tracks, so that if one were to stand up he or she would be looking down onto the tracks.

AnnaLisa and I sat patiently, along with Pastor Kumar, waiting for the train. Pastor Kumar had been excited about this trip into a city where the people were in desperate need to learn about Jesus. AnnaLisa and I knew nothing about the boarding process. We only knew to stay close to Pastor Kumar, who for all intents and purposes was our chaperon. He had the tickets and fares in his hand. I had given him a word that the Lord had given us to insure that AnnaLisa and I sat together during the trip. He assured us that this was all worked out in advance. In fact, the three of us were to travel together in the same train car. After about 20 minutes I heard a train approaching.

I looked and noticed a train headlight approaching in the distance. It was on the opposite set of tracks, about 30 feet across from our platform. I then noticed patrons quickly walking toward the tracks. Amazingly, they were climbing down onto the first set of train tracks in order to cross over to the platform to board the train, which happened to be approaching on the opposite side of where we had been sitting.

AnnaLisa and I looked at each other, both surprised, but relieved. I thought to myself, *"I'm sure glad we're not taking that train."*

Just then I noticed Pastor Kumar jump down onto the tracks and begin running. He made it to the opposite side of the tracks and began yelling to us, "Brother Joel, Sister AnnaLisa, this way…hurry!"

I looked at AnnaLisa and her response was, "You've got to be kidding."

I grabbed her hand and said, "Let's go!"

We were off to the races. Although I was not prepared for this, I knew I was not about to let Pastor Kumar board that train without us. AnnaLisa certainly was not prepared for this. She scuffled, but gamely ran as fast as she could. She happened to be wearing flip-flop sandals at the time, which certainly didn't help matters. Still, I held her hand and we carried baggage as we sprinted, climbing onto and across one set of tracks and then, climbing up to the opposite platform.

The train had now arrived. We were still running, huffing and puffing. Although the train slowed a little it didn't seem to want to stop.

I thought to myself, "*Is this train ever going to stop?*"

To my surprise and dismay, I saw people literally hopping aboard the train. I then saw Pastor Kumar himself hop onto the train.

Frantically he looked back at AnnaLisa and me yelling,

"Hurry, hurry!"

"Well, this is just great," I thought to myself.

186

I knew that the Lord had a specific plan for us to come to India, and the devil certainly was trying to make us quit. I could practically hear the soundtrack of the movie *Indiana Jones* playing as AnnaLisa and I caught up to the car where Pastor Kumar was standing with a bellman, both extending their arms to help us hop aboard.

By the grace of God I was able to hop that train, and of course dear AnnaLisa. Needless to say, I wasn't too happy at that moment with our circumstances.

Once aboard the train, I first took inventory to see if my beloved AnnaLisa was in one piece (and she was - - she didn't even lose her shower sandals -).

Amazingly, we didn't lose any of our gear, no scrapes, no nothing. Just a lot of sweat and a little bit of anger (on my part, at least).

I went to Pastor Kumar and expressed my concern over what had occurred.

But as I began questioning him, he looked at me with a very surprised look on his face and very apologetically said something to the effect of,

'I'm so sorry, Pastor Joel, but this is how the trains run here in India.'

I guess he thought we knew. He was extremely sorry. To make matters worse, his sleeping car was in another coach altogether; when the Lord had said the three of us were to travel together in the same sleep car. To make matters worse still, AnnaLisa and I had separate sleeping areas. I was assigned a sleeping car that only a person no taller than 5' 8" and around 150lbs would be comfortable. I happen to be around 6' 1" 245lbs. I felt like an oversized sardine.

For eight hours on that train I practically had to lie still on my stomach or back, because to lie on my side was nearly impossible due to the height limitation from the mattress to the roof of the sleep car; yes, my bunk was the third bunk, which was on top of two others.

The Lord ministered to me during that ride for sure. At one point He asked me, "Joel, would you like to turn around and go home?" He said, "I will bless you to return home if you like."

The Lord then asked me, "But who would I send in your place, Joel?"

I thought to myself, "*I know God has others to send. I'm honored that He even chose me in the first place.*"

Despite all that was going on, I said without a doubt,

"I'm in it, Lord, all the way."

The Lord then said to me (as He has many times),

"We knew you would say so!"

I came to realize that the Lord had used this episode in order to teach me patience. I also learned that

189

while we may ordinarily expect things to be done in a particular or familiar fashion domestically, such may not be the case when travelling abroad.

The Lord then ministered to AnnaLisa and I (AnnaLisa had a nice *comfortable* sleep car across the aisle from mine on the bottom row).

The Lord assured us that we would see His mighty hand move when we arrived and begin ministering at our destination.

CHAPTER THIRTEEN

IT'S SHRINKING, IT'S SHRINKING!

"And when He had called His twelve disciples to Him, He gave them power over unclean spirits, to cast them out, and to heal all kinds of sickness and all kinds of disease." (Matthew 10:1)

We finally reached our destination and disembarked from the train. Upon arriving at the sanctuary with Pastor Kumar, AnnaLisa and I were introduced to a few other ministers and pastors. The pastors told us that after we ministered our testimony to the congregation, they would like for us to pray for everyone there. Apparently their people had many needs, everything from serious illnesses to routine headaches and backaches, to educational needs for children. We got busy right away doing the business of the Lord.

After the sermon and testimony, the pastors began speaking in their native language and people started lining up in a line that extended from the front of the church to the rear door. Pastor Kumar said to AnnaLisa and I that they were requesting that we pray for them.

There was an interpreter standing by who had interpreted for us during our sermon and testimony. AnnaLisa and I first prayed to the Lord, who told us to begin by asking each person if they believed in Jesus Christ. Now many of the people there were Hindu and believed in many gods, so believing in one more god wasn't a problem for them.

But God had a plan. He was about to show them the difference in believing in just any god, and the One True God. That night several people would be healed. One elderly Hindu man stood gingerly in line holding a cane. He seemed so fragile and appeared to be well into his mid to late seventies, maybe early eighties. As he approached the front of the line, he looked at me with eyes that appeared so deep and heavy with weariness.

His skin was very dark complexioned with a very white contrasting beard, mustache, and eyebrows. I greeted him in English and asked him what his prayer request was? The interpreter translated and the old man spoke in the Telegu Indian dialect. The interpreter told me that this man had cancer. I then noticed the man grab his stomach.

Through his loose flowing shirt I had not noticed that his abdomen was large and distended. It appeared to be the size of a 3-4 month pregnant woman.

Through the promptings of the Holy Spirit I asked the old man through the interpreter if he believed in Jesus Christ. He looked at me with those tired eyes, then closed them and began nodding his head, "Yes."

The Lord then instructed me to lay my hand on his stomach and pray to Jesus to heal him. I touched his stomach with my right hand and began praying. As I prayed, my eyes were closed. Something began to happen. Almost immediately I felt this man trembling and whimpering. I noticed that at first I could easily grip the large tumor. But seconds into praying, it became difficult to maintain my grip. It felt as if the tumor was getting smaller in my grasp making it difficult to get a firm handle on it. I then opened my eyes and repositioned my hand, but the more directly I tried to grab the tumor the smaller it became.

The tumor was incredulously shrinking under my hand right before our eyes! The old man was moaning and crying, not in despair, but for joy.

Realizing that God was performing a miracle in our presence, right under my hands, I began yelling, "It's shrinking! It's shrinking!!"

AnnaLisa joined in and laid her hands on his stomach area also. The two of us prayed for this man until that tumor shrunk down so far that that man's stomach, which minutes ago appeared large enough to contain a small fetus, was normal in size. People cheered and were shocked and amazed.

During the same prayer time, a bearded man who had been waiting for quite a while in line was now at the front of the line. I noticed his arm in a sling. He appeared to possibly be in his mid to late thirties. He asked for prayer, telling me through the interpreter that his arm was fractured. Upon being asked if he believed in Jesus, he said through the interpreter that he did believe in Jesus.

Again, the Lord said to lay my hand on his arm and pray for him. I did as instructed. As I touched this man's arm, I felt the clicking of what seemed to be bones inside of his arm. This continued for a period of seconds. He then left the sanctuary. AnnaLisa and I continued to pray for other people.

The heat was stifling and the two of us must have prayed for at least 100-150 people. We prayed nonstop for about 2 hours. The next day Pastor Kumar told us he had received startling news. Several people apparently had been healed from various illnesses, and Pastor Kumar had been notified.

AnnaLisa and I were scheduled to preach again at a different location that night. When we arrived, I discovered that the man with the broken arm, for whom we had prayed the night before, had showed up at the sanctuary again. When I saw him, he was surrounded by a group of his countrymen. His arm was no longer in a sling.

He was waving his arm wildly about, telling everyone that he had received healing. Apparently, word spread quickly and that night many more people came out. They were lined up for hours. The Lord was communicating with AnnaLisa and me all the while, directing us. That evening we prayed for countless numbers of people.

As we began a second night of praying, I noticed two men carrying a woman into the church. She

195

apparently could not walk and appeared to be stricken with paralysis or some sort of palsy, for lack of a more definitive description of her illness. Needless to say, her legs were not functioning. She was a beautiful woman of about 29 to 35 years of age. Dressed in traditional Indian garb, she was placed in a chair by the two men who were carrying her. Once placed in the chair this woman waited graciously as many others motioned and grabbed at AnnaLisa and me to pray for them or their loved ones. I could barely take my eyes off of this woman. I couldn't help but notice how helpless and withered she appeared to be. Her body was slightly contorted and frail, as if it could snap if pressed too strongly, yet she possessed a radiant smile and her eyes had a glimmer, that shown even through their weary outer appearance.

Meanwhile, the people standing in line for prayer scrambled and pressed against one another anxious to make it to the front of the line. The line progressed slowly. During this time neither this woman, nor the two men who brought her in moved from their position. Still both AnnaLisa and I knew that if there was anyone in the church who truly needed prayer, this woman was the one.

As the line grew shorter, some people began speaking to each other and motioning toward the woman who had been carried in. Soon after, people began stepping aside as if to allow this woman their place, in efforts to usher her to the front of the line. About this time AnnaLisa and I received word from the Lord that He would heal this woman in His time. However, many of the people present had seen God healing people, and had heard about the previous day of miraculous healings. This being the case, they were very adamant about seeing a miracle done in this obviously very impaired woman's life. So although AnnaLisa and I had not planned to approach her just yet, to our surprise the crowd of people insisted we pray for her immediately.

Before we could explain to them about what God had told us, they lifted the chair in which she sat and carried her- chair and all - to the front of the line. Through their native language they insisted that we pray for her to be healed.

The interpreter was saying, "They are asking you to pray for her."

AnnaLisa and I looked at each other. Not knowing what the outcome would be, we began to petition the Lord, praying for her. As we proceeded, I heard someone shout in English, "Stand her up!"

I was not confident that they should move this woman to her feet. I feared that her fragile body would surely crumple if that were done. But before I could even object, two men came forth and stood the woman up. AnnaLisa and I continued praying fervently to God the Father, through our Savior Jesus Christ, to touch this woman's body and heal her, "right now in the name of Jesus."

The woman grabbed my arm and I commanded her to, "Walk, in the name of Jesus!"

She trembled, staring at me with those eyes that appeared both weary, yet wide with hope.

While holding onto me she lifted one leg and took a step. I took a step along with her, telling her to "Walk in Jesus' name."

She appeared to gasp and look back and forth. I then released her grip on me, allowing her to see that she

198

didn't need to lean on me, but to lean on Jesus. She got the message. She took another step and then another. The crowd of people roared in amazement.

AnnaLisa and I were told later that this woman had not walked in five years.

We thanked God for His faithfulness. I learned something that night about God's perfect will and His permissive will. Remember, before encountering this woman, AnnaLisa and I had received a word from the Lord that He would heal her in His time.

Yet, because of the furor and hope of the crowd of people standing by faithfully asking for this woman to be healed, God allowed her to walk that night. In 2 Kings 20, the bible contains an account of God adding 15 years to the life of His servant Hezekiah, even though God had just purposed for Hezekiah to, *Get his house in order* (in other words, to prepare to die). The bible states that Hezekiah, a humble servant of God, was ill and wept bitterly crying out to God, after hearing that the Lord would soon end his life. The Lord then relented, and healed Hezekiah. Hezekiah then lived another 15 years.

God is true to His word, in Hebrews 13:5b He makes a promise to us, *For He Himself Has Said, "I will never leave you nor forsake you."*

The word of God says in Psalm 34:15,

"The eyes of the Lord are on the righteous, and His ears are open to their cry."

AnnaLisa and I had again seen God's faithfulness, as well as His mighty hand moving; this time in India. Between the time that we prepared to leave and return home to California, AnnaLisa and I received several praise reports from people who had been healed of various illnesses, everything from heart disease to cancer. One beautiful young married couple had asked for prayer, as they were trying to have a baby.

They had been unsuccessful for seven years and asked for prayer because they wanted a baby boy. AnnaLisa and I prayed specifically and God said they would have a boy. We informed them that God said it was done. About eight months after returning to California, we received correspondence from the elated couple telling us that they were indeed having a baby boy, nearly nine months after the prayer. Coincidence? Not hardly! It was God doing what He does.

Pastor Kumar was so thrilled to see the amazing miracles God had performed in India. He attempted to correspond with the senior pastor of our church, both by letter and email, in order to share the wonderful news of God's miraculous healings. Unfortunately, our pastor would not even respond to or even acknowledge Pastor Kumar's letters.

Pastor Kumar could not understand how a pastor of a church could deny allowing such a powerful testimony of the greatness of God to be told to his sheep.

As the Bible states in Rev 12:11,

"They overcame him by the blood of the Lamb and the word of their testimony."

God gives obedient servants testimonies to be shared in order to edify the body, and advance the kingdom of God to exalt the name of Jesus, and Jesus' name alone. To show that, as it was with the original church of Macedonia in the book of Acts, God is willing to do the same things in His churches today. The church

201

today would do itself a tremendous service if it would not just **read** God's word, but **plead** God's word, **bleed** God's word, and ***truly believe*** God's word. Our leaders must learn to not put God in a box. For He blesses whom He blesses, and curses whom He curses. He does as He pleases and will use those whose hearts are truly turned to Him.

Undaunted by non-support from our church pastorate AnnaLisa and I continued serving the Lord. Even under contentious circumstances we were buffeted by the Lord's words that a prophet is not welcome in his own home. Meanwhile, God didn't miss a beat. The praise reports from India continued to come in. God continued to elevate us and prepare us for more work in His kingdom. Isaiah 55:11 tells us that God's word goes out and does not return to Him void. The Lord says of His word,

"It shall accomplish what I please. It shall prosper in the thing for which I sent it."

I know this to be true. For although we were obviously challenged by dark forces in our own home church, attempting to restrain God's miraculous works from being revealed to the church, true believers sought us out. People would approach AnnaLisa and me in church, hungry for news of modern day accounts of the miraculous moves and majesty of the Living God. Excitedly they would come and invite us to share with them the wondrous works that God had done during our assignments.

We were, and are yet humbled that we have been chosen to be vessels of honor for the Most High.

CHAPTER FOURTEEN

TAKING IT TO THE STREETS!

Jesus' great commission is that we make disciples of all the nations. And although AnnaLisa and I were sent abroad quite early in our walk with Christ, we realize that our missionary assignment includes the U.S, every state, every city, every school, every church, and wherever we find ourselves with an opportunity to share the Gospel of Christ.

God continued to use us, as soon as approximately 1 year after our returning home from India; God sent us on another assignment, this time to Guyana, South America. AnnaLisa and I were paired with a team of sold out, Holy Ghost filled pastors, bent on serving the Lord by spreading the Gospel, and making disciples of all the nations. Pastor Don Whitney and his wife Maria Whitney, Pastor Verna Brown and her daughter (Children's Minister, Simone Brown) and Pastors Dana and Mitch Waller all traveled to the jungles of Guyana's interior with us.

Arriving in Guyana, a country where the practice of voodoo and the occult is rampant, we met with Pastor

Rodwell McClean and his lovely wife Grace, and proceeded to be about our Father's business of spreading the Word of God in impoverished places where there abounds lost souls needing to be saved. Hallelujah!

In the neighborhood where Pastor McClean resides, several graves had been dug up and the bodies of loved ones desecrated with heads removed and stolen in efforts by grave robbers to cast demonic spells on surviving relatives. So prevalent in this country are the demonic works of the enemy that the Pastor informed us that at least 5 Christian ministers in his neighborhood had fled their residences and apparently their positions in the body of Christ in fear for their lives due to demonic oppression. And I must say that while it is not my intent to question the resolve of these purported ministers of the Gospel who allegedly fled when faced with the demonic.

I stand firmly on the truth of the Holy Bible; that *"God has not given us a spirit of fear, but power, love and a sound mind."* (2 Timothy 1:7)

I am happy to report that not only were demons cast out in Guyana, but people were saved and came to the knowledge of Christ Jesus. Our group operated

206

largely in the jungles of Guyana, in places accessible only by boat amid piranha and python infested waters.

Still the word of God penetrated and the inhabitants of this harsh and impoverished area benefited from the power of God through the word of God. The things that were accomplished in Guyana certainly did not occur from my or my wife's strength, or the strength of our comrades whom we accompanied, but through the power of the Holy Spirit in the name of Jesus Christ.

I John 4:4 reminds us that,

"You are of God little children, and have overcome them, because He who is in you is greater than he who is in the world."

No matter how sinister or bleak things may appear in the natural, we as Christ followers have to know and truly believe that we have an all-powerful God who goes before us.

"And God is able to make all grace abound to you, so that having all sufficiency in all things at all times, you may abound in every good work." (II Corinthians 9:8). That is the power and grace of God!

207

Upon our return to the U.S., God continued to do the miraculous, informing AnnaLisa and I that we would become pastors of a church to be named Spirit of Truth Church Worldwide. We certainly had no ideas or plans to pastor a church. We had just assumed that we would continue spending our time spreading God's word as missionaries and psalmists for the Lord, since at the time that is what God had revealed to us. But God is omniscient. He is all wise and all knowing. He knew long before He called me in 2004 that if I had known what His overall plan was for me, I probably would have been overwhelmed, and may have been tempted to run the other way; especially when He informed us that we would pastor a church.

Pastor AnnaLisa and I now realize that God has even bigger plans for us. As I continue to pen the amazing details of this book, bringing this excerpt to an end, God is steadily moving in our lives. Things are moving so briskly, occurring by His Divine will and Spirit that we can barely keep up with the events.

Not only have AnnaLisa and I been *On the Job With God* in the church and abroad, but He has seen fit to continually place me in new situations. God continues to perform miracles, assisting me on calls in and around the streets of San Francisco, the Bay area and beyond, just as He has done with His servants in locations throughout the Holy Bible.

Time and time again when confrontations have arrived during the course of performing my daily law enforcement duties, Jesus has shown up right there in the heat of the battle, to turn certain disaster into victory. Whether I have been forced to square off with a 300lb violent offender who just recently had easily handled up to 8 officers; or called upon by God to save a man or woman on a rain slicked rooftop who decided that leaping off that roof to their death was their best option. To saving me from having to take the life of a demon possessed man who was convinced that he was a werewolf and had cannibalized portions of his two children, to making arrests of dangerous armed felons without ever having to draw a weapon! Jesus was there each and every time to take over the scene. He is the best partner a street cop could ever have.

Clear and honest stories like these and more will be chronicled and shared when the Lord opens the door in the near future in the next edition of *On the Job With God (Taking It To The Streets)*.

Now what about you? You see, it's not mandatory that you be a police officer in order to be on the job with God. That's just part of the prescription He used in my case in order for me to enter into this amazing relationship with Him. You can do the same, regardless of where you are in your life right now.

If you happen to be where I was (just 8 years ago) and do not truly know Him, just ask Jesus to come into your life, repent your sins to Him and allow Him to guide you. You will then be a candidate to go to work with Jesus. He will train you, prepare you, and direct you in the job that He has planned for you. Until then, please continue to seek God in everything you do. Remember God sent His only begotten Son to die for you (John 3:16).

He has invested in you and wants a return on His investment. God is ready to work with you. The question is, are you ready to work with Him? Are you ready to be *On the Job With God*?

AUTHOR BIO

Joel Jones was born and raised in Chicago, IL. Joel is the 12th of 13 children born to Thomas and Mary Jones. Joel's parents were devout followers of the Nation of Islam. They reared their children in the teachings of this Islamic group. However, it was Joel's older siblings who received the strictest teachings of Islam. God allowed Joel to excel in sports, which provided the opportunity for Joel to receive a full scholarship to a major university in Des Moines, IA. Leaving Chicago at the age of 18, allowed Joel to escape the teachings of this man-made religion.

Joel left Chicago and soon sent for Denise, and started his own family. After a brief opportunity to play professional football, Joel settled into working as a police officer in the State of California in order to provide for his family. And while he did the best he could to show them the way, his efforts were inadequate because Joel did not know God. He didn't believe in Christianity, nor did he believe in Jesus. As a matter of fact, Joel had never sat down and read a Bible or attended church services before the age of forty-nine. Well, in 2004 Joel and Denise simultaneously received a major supernatural epiphany, complete with the sighting of angels and an ultimate meeting with Christ Himself. Both were taken up in the Spirit for six consecutive days, escorted by the Lord of Lords, and King of kings. Needless to say, their lives were changed, for the better...forever. God had a magnificent plan, but not only to change Joel's life for the better, but the lives of his family, his friends, and all who read this book and seek a true relationship with Jesus Christ.

Joel Jones is now Pastor Joel Jones. His wife Denise is now Pastor AnnaLisa Jones. Both are prayer warriors who continue to see the mighty hand of God moving in their lives. Both are also gospel songwriters and recording artists with ASCAP. They have ministered across the U.S. and abroad: in South Africa, India and South America. They are the founders of Spirit of Truth Church Worldwide, a church only 3 years in its development, based in Crockett, CA. Their broadcasts can currently be heard on Saturday mornings at 10:30 AM on KDYA radio 1190, and Sunday mornings at 10:30 AM on KDIA radio 1640.

A JOURNEY
THROUGH TIME

FEATURED
HIGGINS PUBLISHING BOOKS

ON THE JOB WITH GOD: *TAKING IT TO THE STREETS*
BY JOEL JONES – *(COMING SOON)*

MY LIFE JOURNAL BIBLE STUDY (A SERIES)
BY SHANENE HIGGINS

WOMAN OF PURPOSE, POWER AND PASSION
AN ANTHOLOGY OF HOPE & DIRECTION

A ROMANCE WITH THE MASTER
BY KAREN D. GREENWELL

MY ALABASTER BOX
BY DORIS COLLIS

HIGGINS PUBLISHING
P.O. BOX 22785
OAKLAND, CA 94609
PH: 510-431-6832

HTTP://WWW.HIGGINSPUBLISHING.COM

218

SPEAKING ENGAGEMENTS

To Schedule Joel Jones for upcoming speaking engagements, visit: HIGGINSPUBLISHING.COM, or call: 510-431-6832.

BOOK REVIEW SUBMITTAL

If this book has been a blessing to you, submit a review online at our website, or at your favorite bookstore.

Thank you for taking the time

to let us know how you enjoyed this book!

ON THE JOB WITH GOD: THE AWAKENING

ORDER FORM

THREE WAYS TO ORDER

ORDER ONLINE AT
HTTP://WWW.HIGGINSPUBLISHING.COM
COPY & FAX THIS ORDER FORM TO: 1-877-937-2250

MAIL THIS ORDER FORM TO:
HIGGINS PUBLISHING, P.O. BOX 22785
OAKLAND, CA 94609

CUSTOMER CONTACT INFORMATION:
NAME:_____
ADDRESS: _____
CITY:_____STATE:_____ZIP: _____
PHONE:_____CELL: _____
EMAIL: _____
BILLING INFORMATION:
CREDIT CARD#:_____
EXPIRATION:_____CVV2#:____

TOTAL COPIES REQUESTED AT: $24.95/ea: _____
TOTAL AMOUNT ENCLOSED: $ _____

*** All sales are final ***

SIGNATURE:_____

Please note tax and shipping will be added to your order
upon processing if applicable.
** Please allow up to 15 days for delivery **
Thank You for Your Order!

CPSIA information can be obtained
at www.ICGtesting.com
Printed in the USA
BVOW10*0904140717

488852BV00003B/7/P